SYSTEMA
SELF DEFENCE

Robert Poyton

Published by Cutting Edge

ISBN 978-1-7399855-2-3

ABOUT THE AUTHOR

Robert was born in the early 1960's in East London.
He trained in Judo and boxing as a child and at age
18 began training in Yang Family Taijiquan.

For many years he studied the Chinese Internal Arts in depth.
In the 1990's he set up his own school and began cross
training in several styles.

In 2000 he began training in Systema and has since trained
extensively with with Mikhail Ryabko and Vladimir Vasiliev in both
Moscow and Toronto. In addition he has arranged numerous UK
seminars for Mikhail, Vladimir and other instructors.

Robert now trains solely in Systema and runs regular classes
in the UK and teaches seminars throughout the UK and Europe.
He has been featured in numerous martial arts books and magazines
as well as producing his own publications and training films.

Outside of training, Robert is a professional musician and currently
lives in rural Bedfordshire with his wife and a small menagerie.

*"Rob Poyton has been training and teaching Systema since 2000.
He is a dedicated and talented instructor, knowledgeable on
all of the key components of Systema. Rob presents his teaching
in a clear and structured manner through his classes
and reading materials."*
- Vladimir Vasiliev, October 2019.

Dedicated to
the memory of
David Flaherty:
a truly fine teacher
and gentleman

CONTENTS

CHAPTER ONE
INTRODUCTION

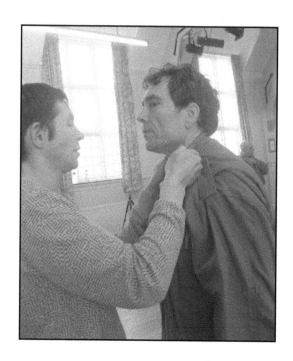

If you took a poll asking people "why did you take up martial arts?" I'm betting that the top, or at least one of the top three, answers would be *"self defence."* It may be that people have had a bad experience - being bullied, robbed, etc. It may be that they have concerns about crime in their local area and wish to learn how to protect themselves and their families. The person could be a professional, perhaps in security, an LEO, working in a facility of some kind and so on. Other people enjoy the physicality of this type of training, they may enjoy fighting, whether from a sports of other perspective. Whatever the individual reason, self defence is a major reason for people to begin training in martial arts.

Now, when it comes to martial arts there are countless schools available - from Renaissance sword fighting schools to modern military combative classes and everything in-between. In fact the beginner may find the choice overwhelming! The stereotypical view of people high-kicking and chopping in "pyjamas" probably still remains but there is, today, an incredibly wide choice, a far cry from those who remember the "old days" when it was pretty much only judo, karate and boxing.

Systema, though it has roots dating back into the distant past, is a relatively modern school, first taught outside of Russia by Vladimir Vasiliev in the early 1990s. Systema means *the System* and I use it here to refer specifically to the school and method founded by Mikhail Ryabko, Vladimir's teacher. The term is now used in rather the same way as *Kung-fu* is for Chinese styles, to refer to many different types of Russian martial art. However, most of those trace back either to Ryabko or Kadochnikov, with some exceptions.

Whether Systema is a "martial art" is a debate for another time, as it has a radically different approach from the more familiar Eastern styles. However, there is no doubt that self defence is an large element of Systema, and a reason that many people take it up. I'm assuming that readers of this book will have at least some familiarity of the art, if not, I recommend many of the other good books available on Systema, or to search on-line for videos and articles for more information. To that end, I'll forego any introduction about its background, core principles and general methods, and get straight into our subject matter - self defence.

The first thing, then, is to define our terms. I want to be very clear about what I mean here by self defence. In general, I view self defence training as any practice that increases our chances of survival / escape from harm in any situation. That includes the obvious fights, arguments, etc, but also includes any dangerous incident or accident, as well as protecting ourselves from other dangers - sickness, illness,

disease, both physical and mental.

In that sense, then, the scope of self defence practice is extremely broad, and, fortunately for us, Systema has both breadth and depth! Its methods of physical protection also happen to be good for our health and fitness. And, of course, there are numerous health-specific methods within general Systema training.

This is great but it does present a problem for anyone writing a book, teaching, or presenting any material about Systema - and that is how to structure the training. If we were extremely talented, marvellous people we could, perhaps, study everything at once. However, most of us struggle with one or two things at a time, and so we "slice" our training down into component parts.

These include basic concepts, such as the Four Pillars, each of which can be trained separately; specific techniques, such as

applying a lock or hold; general attributes, such as balance, strength; or task-orientated skills such as close protection work, the use of weapons, and so on. We may also break our training down into small slices of time, such as the second a strike impacts, or so on. Now, even then there is considerable cross-over and separation in training is always a construct or compromise. Nonetheless, this slicing of training allows us to more easily take in and digest the information we receive from our teachers.

This, to me, is another strength of Systema, doing away, as it does, with the need for set moves, kata, forms, or a rigid syllabus. The downside is that the newcomer, both to learning and teaching, can feel a little overwhelmed in knowing where to start (hint- *it's always with breathing!*)

So, back to self defence! For the purposes of this book I am focusing on what I would call "general, every day physical self defence." In other words, the type of situation we might, with a bit of bad luck, find ourselves in as we go about our business. Road rage, a drunk in a pub, a street thief, a workplace bully and so on.

To that end, I will not be covering what I term *professional work,* ie various types of close protection work, bouncers, security, LEO, military, etc. Naturally, there is cross-over, but there are also some specifics to those topics that I will address in another book. I'm also not going to focus too much on dealing with edged and other weapons. Again, that is another book in itself - for example Vladimir Vasiliev's excellent *Edge.*

Lastly, I'm not covering some of the more unlikely or even borderline fantasy scenarios that form the basis of much speculation on the internet - defence against Ninjas, how to take out a biker gang, being the so-called "alpha male" guardian of the "sheeple" and so on.

Again, I'm sticking to real-world situations, where our prime focus is on protecting ourselves in order to *escape.* And that brings me on to my next point.

It is very common in books on self defence to see what I call the *photo romance* approach. By that, I mean a series of photos that tell a little story. The photos are usually highly staged and recount some type of attack, say a mugger trying to hit

you with an iron bar. There then follows a series of instructions along the lines of "place your left foot forward, and block upwards with your right arm." By following these precise moves, you overcome the attacker and go about your day. This is an attractive method of learning for some, as it offers a neat, easy solution to a horrible problem.

Unfortunately, real life is rarely so neat and easy. There are many more factors in a real life event beyond where you place your hands and feet. Awareness, fear management, the physical ability to carry out the technique, the ability to adapt, dealing with consequences, all of these and more must be considered in our approach. When you look at it from this perspective, learning set patterns and techniques

becomes more of a liability than an assistance.

This step-by-step approach also leads to people thinking that by reading a technique, they have learnt it. That in a situation, this intellectual knowledge will somehow spring forth. Alas, this is not the case. The work presented here is work to be *done*. I will explain later on how to work drills to develop the skills - in other words, this book is not a loaf of bread, but it will teach you how to bake one!

This book will generally discuss principle over technique - in other words, the usual Systema approach. So if you are looking for a "how to" manual of moves, this may not be the book for you. However, if you are looking to become adaptable, effective in every stage of a situation and, importantly, balanced in your approach, then I hope you will find some useful ideas here.

Alongside this, I'm taking another different approach to "conventional" self defence books, and that is to ground all of our work and examples in actual events. Every incident in this book actually happened - either to me or to a friend, colleague, or student. This includes what we might consider successes and failures. This is not a book of war stories, there's no talk of having hundreds of street fights or of being hard as nails. These are the experiences of ordinary people who found themselves in a particular situation - in some cases when young, in some when much older!

They include times both pre and post Systema training and so represent people of different experience levels. I have tried to include a range of experiences, some of them are not even what you might think of as a "fight." Nonetheless, they are situations that induced stress and had at least the threat of physical danger. I'd also like to add that no judgement is passed on the people involved. You may find actions described in some of the accounts distasteful, or you may think them "wrong." Regardless, these are events that actually happened and my sole concern for the purposes of this book is what we can take from these experiences in order to improve our training.

This approach is mirrored in our classes. Students bring experiences to the group, we talk them through and discuss / practice various ways of solving the problem. This helps keeps our training fresh, grounded in reality and specific for the sort of situations people might be involved in. This is important, as needs may change according to time and place. Take door work, for example. I did a little of this back in London in the 1980s

which, by all accounts, was a very different time and place to door work now (and probably for the good.)

So this is how the book works. In the first half, we recount situations from the point of view of the person directly involved. After that, we will pick out some of the key points and suggest drills or strategies that may have helped. Of course, there are numerous common points throughout, but I will focus on just one or two specifics per incident.

In the second half of the book, we will cover ways of structuring our training in order to combine all these different aspects into a coherent approach. Some of this is an expansion of methods from a previous book, *The Ten Points of Sparring.* I will stick to direct methods here as much as possible, so won't be overly detailing supplementary areas of training such as strength, mobility, etc, none of which, of course, should be neglected.

I will also skirt a little over topics covered

in detail in my previous books - where required, I'll point you to those. As I always say, no single volume can cover every single situation, technique, attribute and so on. Think of this book, then, as giving you a framework on which to hang all those other attributes and skills.

How you use this book is up to you. You may wish to read through the whole book, then pick out some specific ideas for training drills. You may wish to recreate one of the incidents, then have a go at some of the suggestions we make. Of course, I also encourage you to examine your own experiences and draw from them accordingly. Either way, I sincerely hope you find the material here useful, whether in teaching or, God forbid, in actual use.

In closing, I'd like to thank my teachers, Mikhail Ryabko and Vladimir Vasiliev, whose outstanding methods and advice I attempt to replicate here. Also, a big thanks to all my regulars for being so generous in sharing experiences, and assisting with photographs.

CHAPTER TWO
AWARENESS

Our first two incidents are something many people will have experienced, street robbery. We will use them to look at ideas around awareness and spotting trouble before it spots you. Let's begin.

STREET ROBBERY

I was about eight years old and on my way home from school. A pair of older lads suddenly confronted me, blocking my way. They were older boys, aged 14 or so. One of them said, "give me your money or I'll stab you." He waved a compass in my face - not the direction type, but the pointy thing you use to draw circles, a standard part of maths kits at the time! I gave him my money (which wasn't very much), they moved aside and I ran home.

This was a not uncommon occurrence in those days. It happened to me a few times in different places - the park, outside school, etc. Later on it became known as being "mugged" or "taxing," and developed to having your smart top or trainers nicked as well as money. Two things struck me in that particular case.

First, those kids weren't the smartest. I had more money on the way to school than on the way home. Dinner money, for a start. The second thing was how open and blatant it was but also how easy it was to see coming. Crossing the road mostly avoided the situation, or taking another route home. The other solution was to travel in groups, these robbers rarely bothered a group of other kids, even if they were smaller. Like most thieves, they didn't want a big scene or fuss. Just in, threaten, and away.

The other solution of course, was if you had a big brother or something. Telling a teacher didn't do much, they could only really operate on school premises. None of us ever thought to go the police, it wasn't really the done thing. Same with your parents - in fact one mate of mine got told off by his dad for allowing himself to get robbed! Maybe that's a reason boxing classes were so popular thing once you reached a certain age?

Ask instructors what the fundamental self defence skill is and they will almost all respond with *awareness*. Knowing what is going on around us, spotting potential trouble, being self-aware and so on are vital attributes. In this situation, we see how there was a lack of awareness to being with. The boy was suddenly confronted, he hadn't spotted the older boys approach. However, after the incident, we see that he upped his awareness game. Once bitten, he was aware of the how these robbers operated and so it became quite easy to avoid them. Simply being aware of the potential threat, changing a route, walking in a group and so on helped a lot with avoidance.

The second thing to take from this incident is that turning to an authority had little effect. Now, I don't doubt if there had been a police officer around at the time, that would have been a different situation. Post-incident, however, it seems there would be little that could be done. Also, as the person mentioned, the teacher had limited authority in that situation. It's interesting that the other type of "authority" to turn to is the older sibling, or similar - in effect, getting a bodyguard! We can think of this from both directions, in fact one of the best reasons to learn Systema is to help protect others.

Awareness, then, can mean being cognisant of our immediate surroundings and situation. But it can also be applied longer term, by being prepared. A little forethought, particularly if we know what threat we might face, can help. That could range from carrying a personal alarm through to having some friends with you or, as the narrator mentions, taking up some kind of self defence method, be it boxing, martial arts, or learning how to run fast! Let's look at another robbery incident.

BAG SNATCH

I had taken my elderly mother on a holiday abroad. We were in a large city and took a short-cut down a quiet side street. About halfway down I heard my mother make a noise. I turned, and a man had jumped off the back of a moped and was trying to pull my mother's handbag from her grasp. For a second I froze, I couldn't believe what was happening! Then I jumped forward to also hold onto the bag straps. In doing so, my own handbag slid down my arm and the robber grabbed that one too. By now, my mother had let go, so I was in a tug of war with the robber. He was stronger than me and he pulled me off balance, virtually dragging me across the pavement. He leapt back on the pillion with both bags and the driver zoomed off.

Another situation, then, where the people were caught unaware. Could it have been avoided? Perhaps, with some forethought. Moving out of a tourist area into a quieter place might not be advisable, particularly if you are in a city that has known crime issues. Another question is, why were both people carrying handbags? Were they really required, or was this just a habit? If required, maybe a handbag could be tucked under a jacket, or held close to the body. We also have the question of the approach of the robber, in this case by moped. The moped actually came up onto the pavement, which should be an instant indication of potential danger.

Another interesting point in this case is that the daughter first froze on seeing what was happening. This is not an uncommon issue and is something we shall address in a future chapter. Lastly, there was more than one person involved, in this case someone elderly. This goes back to our bodyguard idea - we may find ourselves in a situation where our main concern is another person's safety, which will obviously influence our actions.

AWARENESS

For an in-depth study of the subject, I refer you to our *Systema Awareness* book. But in terms of both situations above, here are some things to consider:

1. Be aware of where you are - is it known as a rough or dangerous area?

2. Be aware of who you are - do you stand out, or look like a tourist? Are you obviously carrying money or expensive items?

3. Scan ahead - be aware of any groups or people loitering. Are they watching you? If so, can you avoid them - cross over the road, take another route, etc.

4. Look at body language, listen to your inner voice - if it feels dangerous, it most likely is.

5. If confronted, have a plan. For example, in what circumstances would you hand over your property, in what circumstances would you resist, try to talk your way out or try and escape? Of course, as the saying goes, no plan survives contact with the enemy, but having a plan is a solid base to work from and explore your options.

6. Scan around. Don't get tunnel vision. If you think someone is following you, cross the road, go into a shop, or whatever you can do to evade.

7. What do you project? Tests have shown that street criminals tend to target those who look vulnerable. As the first narrator said, they don't want a fuss, just a quick and easy job. If you look like a person who could cause problems, that may act as a deterrent. Don't think that means you must be seven feet tall

and built like Arnie. Confidence is the major attribute here and that comes from inside. Not being aggressive, not walking around with your chest puffed out - that usually incites trouble. But giving an air of knowing what you are about, making eye contact with a steady gaze, being smooth and compact in your movement, all contribute to the aura of confidence.

Ironically acting like a "crazy person" might also have the same effect, ie being very visible and vocal in your action. Even robbers want a quiet life! The other side of that is to be the proverbial "grey person." To blend in so well that you go largely unnoticed. If you look like you fit in the area and are not obviously vulnerable, your chances of being left alone improve.

8. If you are with other people, a child, an elderly relative or so on, involve them in your training. At the very least, talk to them about what may happen and, again, have

a plan formed. It may be as simple as "if we get separated, meet up at the hot dog stand." It may be more involved, in a physical sense. In essence, learn to be your own bodyguard. Teach your family about awareness. You don't want to overly scare them, but do make them aware of any potential dangers they may face.

If all goes well with the above, then we can avoid the robbery situation. If we do get confronted though, what should we do? It is very difficult to give general advice that applies to every situation. Let's look at some of the factors we have to take into consideration.

1. Who are the attackers? In both cases above, the robbers were youngsters. Probably not likely to go beyond the threatening stage, though that can be a difficult thing to judge. If, on the other hand, the robber is a person with severe issues, they may not be working under the same set of rules as "normal" people. Whatever the cause of their condition, they may not even view you as a person, with a corresponding lack of empathy or care for consequences of their actions.

2. What is the environment? Are there other people around? You can' always rely on help from others but you can, at least, make a fuss and noise, draw attention to what is going on.

3. How attached are you? What will they get from you? A few coins, or that expensive watch your wife bought you for your 40th birthday? A cheap phone or the latest all-singing, all -dancing I-whatever? In different places, at different times, demands may change. In our example, it was cash. At other times, people would rob trainers or portable stereos. Cash is still probably the favourite, for obvious reasons, but an addict desperate to score will take anything they think they can sell.

4. What happens next? If you give the items, will the person then leave you alone. I would say this is generally the case but can you rely on that? In some instances, a person may still attack you even after getting "the goods." On the other hand, if you resist, are you prepared for the consequences - the violence that will ensue and it's possible aftermath of police involvement, the risk of injury or death (on both sides)?

AWARENESS DRILLS

Go for a walk around your neighbourhood. The exercise will do you good! Leave your phone at home, don't listen to any music. Plan out a 20 minute route, you can work ladder breathing or similar in too. Take time to look around. Are there things you pass every day that you haven't noticed before? Stop and look if you need to, there's no rush.

Another option is to play I-Spy with

yourself. How many things can you see that begin with the letter B? How many red objects can you see on your walk? Train yourself to notice things, to be observant.

Extend this out to whenever you are walking or driving (if safe to do so). You can also use the commentary method. As you go, the aim is to keep up a running verbal commentary of what you see around you. This helps keeps the mind focused.

The next drill works best with a group, such as in class. Have the group work together for a while, as normal. Now have one person leave the room or turn their back. The others must make some change to their appearance - swap tee shirts, put on gloves, etc. The person now returns and must see if they can spot the changes.

There are many variations on this theme. You can change something about the room - move a chair, etc. You can suddenly stop the training and ask questions - "without

as our first examples highlight. I remember in younger days, being very aware of which area I was walking in (in terms of rival gangs) and of being "tuned in" to sensing the approach of violence. There is quite often a build up to a violent situation. I always find that in certain circumstances, say a social gathering or in a crowd, it is quite easy to detect this. I guess that attribute comes from experience and innate survival instinct, but it can be enhanced with training. Here's a few pointers to watch out for.

looking, what colour socks is Sam wearing?" and so on. The aim is to get people using their awareness on an everyday level, not just when doing an awareness exercise.

If you have the time and facilities, you can extend this to outside the class. If practical, have one of your group attempt to follow or approach unseen another at some time. Remember, the aim is not to make people paranoid and jumpy but to increase their natural awareness. This is something we all have but it tends to get dampened down by modern, urban living.

SENSING TROUBLE

I tend to find that people with a more outdoor lifestyle are generally more aware of their environment, particularly in terms of weather and wildlife. However the same principles apply to the urban setting, too,

1. Changes in volume - usually raised voices, or an increase in the general crowd sound. Next time you are in a crowd, close your eyes and listen. There's normally a hum of conversation going on. In the old days it was often depicted as people going "rhubarb, rhubarb, rhubarb." Listen for any raised single voice and listen for a change in tone or volume in the general hum. If there is a situation, people around often stop talking to turn and look. Or you may hear an intake of breath after something happens. In football days you'd often hear the sound of running feet and chants as a precursor to trouble. Basically, be aware of any changes in sound.

2. Situational awareness - be aware of who is around you and why they are there.

Pickpockets like to operate in crowds, especially on tube trains. Easy to approach, easy to slip away, the crowd is urban camouflage. But there are indicators to watch for. Is everyone else wearing a blue football top and you a red one? As mentioned before, are you an obvious tourist or outsider?

Monitor your own behaviour, especially in terms of volume levels. Why draw attention to yourself if you don't need to? You may also need to park your ego. If someone bumps into you, slip away, you don't have to react. Of course, there are methods for working in crowds, which we will talk about later on, but generally speaking, work to blend in.

3. Who is in the room - when you go into a bar, club or similar, have a quick scan round. I don't mean stare everyone in the eye, that can lead to problems! Just have a quick look. Who's around? Who looks like potential trouble? Who's the security? Also note where the exits are, how is the room arranged where the pool cues are, and so on. Again, just a glance, a natural scan, that's all that's needed

4. What are you presenting - how do you enter a room? What messages do your posture and appearance give off? Imagine going into a new pub, barrel chested, flinging the door open,

pausing in the doorway and glaring around. In some parts of the world that's an instant invitation. We used to call it the Stratford Pub Quiz, question one "who do you think you are?" Question two "do you want some?"

5. Who else is coming in - I watched a documentary on Youtube about a group of middle-aged, professional men who were trying to be a biker group in the USA. They stopped over at one particular bar and a few minutes later a small group of Hells Angels turned up. Their leader came in first. He was an old dude, silver hair and beard, but he walked into that place like a big wolf leading the pack. He was smiling, he paused, openly clocked everyone in the room, then strode slowly to the bar. The mild-life crisis biker guys visibly shrank in their seats, it's one of the best entrances I've ever seen (you can see it on the *HA Prison Run* YT channel.)

I've experienced similar when a known "face" comes into the room, or it may be a

item close by, or stand next to it. A chair or table can make an effective shield, for example.

UNDERSTANDING BODY LANGUAGE

The above all work largely on the big picture but we should also look at situations where people are right in front of us. In these cases it is useful to have some knowledge of body language. Most of our communication is non-verbal. Unless highly trained, people are unable to disguise their intentions or emotions, they tend to manifest physically in some way. The most obvious example would be an angry person - the face contorts and becomes reddened, the chest puffs up, the arms splay out. All good indicators of potential violence.

Again, this is a very wide and deep subject and I refer you to *Systema Awareness* for a more complete guide. Here are some general pointers, though.

FEET

The zoologist Desmond Morris observed that the feet reveal our feelings more honestly than any other part of the body! Check which direction the feet are pointing. A foot turned away tends to indicate a desire to leave the situation. People in a good mood may jiggle or bounce their feet. Foot tapping, may indicate impatience.

Our legs are primarily used for walking and there are a whole host of indicators in

famous person, you can sense the change in atmosphere.

6. Atmosphere - this really is the best guide of all. Develop a feeling for reading the mood of a room, or a group of people. Watch for the signs above, plus agitated behaviour, prolonged eye contact, and so on. Most performers, particularly comedians, have this down to a fine art and the best can often manipulate or direct the mood of a crowd in some way.

7. Have a plan - as we mentioned before, it's a good idea to have a plan, however simple it may be. In fact, the simpler the better. If you've noted where the exits are, in case of trouble, you can position yourself to be quickly out of the place. If you have people or children with you, let them know to follow your lead. Or your plan may be to use something to hand, so you place the

the way a person walks. Watch for any obvious tension and observe the general posture. Hunched or straight? Speed is important, too. Nervous people tend to speed up. Someone carefree may breeze along, taking in their surroundings as they go.

Walking can also be a good measure of intention. You should be able to spot the person from across a room who comes barrelling over to punch you in the face! On the other hand (or foot) watch how friends approach and greet each other. Sometimes there is a little dance, followed by a handshake or hug. A walk may also be an indicator of concealed weapons, so watch to see if the walker is tense in one spot, almost as though trying to conceal something with the posture.

TORSO

The torso contains most of our vital organs – heart, lungs, kidneys, etc. Perhaps for this reason the usual behaviour of a stressed torso is to create distance. One example of this is the "torso lean" that you may observe in some social situations. The person feels they cannot get up and walk away, but the body will lean away from the offending party. Another version of this is blading. This is where the torso is turned at a slight angle from the perceived threat.

Fronting is a more aggressive action. We actually used to call it "fronting someone up." The chest is puffed out, the arms splayed. A classic territorial display, it may even lead to chest bumping and what has become known as the "monkey dance," where two people want to show they are willing to fight but might not really actually want to yet! It's also not uncommon to see the torso bared in these situations, men ripping off their shirts as part of the display.

Covering the torso with the arms may be pacifying behaviour, though it can also be a method of shielding or blocking. Chest shielding is generally more prominent in women, for obvious reasons, perhaps, but men will exhibit the same - crossing an arm over the body to fiddle with a cufflink, for example.

ARMS

Our shoulders are quite expressive. Think how often you use them in communication. A shrug that says "I don't know," or perhaps even "I don't care!" Sometimes the shoulders

train seat, or spread their arms across the chairs on each side of them?

Another variation is the "hands on hips" stance, with elbows pushed out to the side. This is usually a display of authority. One last arm position is where the hands are held behind the head. People often do this while leaning back in their chair. It is called "hooding" and can be a display of authority. It is interesting to note that if someone with greater authority enters the space, the hands are immediately removed back down to normal position!

rise slowly. This is known as "turtling" almost as though the person is trying to withdraw into their shell. It's usually a sign of discomfort or of not wanting to be associated with whatever is going on.

Shielding by crossing the arms is usually an indicator of dislike or discomfort. By contrast, when happy or joyful we tend to raise our arms, as though defying gravity. As a rough guide, think hands up happy, hands down, sad.

Hands behind the back can show confidence, as in the "Royal stance". They may also be saying "don't come close." You can think of it as a reverse hug. Of course, in a self defence context, concealed hands may also indicate potential weapon threat.

Arms are also used in territorial displays. We have mentioned the "chest puffed, arms wide" stance but there are more subtle actions too. Ever jostled for the arm rest on a flight? Have you seen how some people spread themselves across a

FACE

The most expressive part of our body and the one we observe the most in order to gauge another person's emotions. There are an estimated ten thousand human facial expressions and, for the most part, they are universal across all cultures. We can, to a degree, control our facial muscles, so the face may not always be the best indicator. Having said that, there is something called *micro-expressions* that we can watch out for.

Micro-expressions are very brief, involuntary expressions that appear on a person's face according to the emotions being experienced. They usually occur as fast as 1/15 to 1/25 of a second. Unlike regular expressions, they are difficult to fake.

There are seven universal micro-expressions: disgust, anger, fear, sadness, happiness, surprise and contempt.

I'm sure you are able to recognise each of those - the brows knit for anger, the lips turn up for a smile for happiness, down for sadness and so on. The trick is to catch these expressions as they occur. A person attempting to mask their emotions will quickly regain control of the muscles to present whatever it is they wish to project. However, that little flash of honesty may give the game away, so watch out for them!

Negative emotions create tension. Brows furrow, jaws clench, nostrils flare, lips press together. When happy, our faces tend to "open" more. We smile, our eyes widen, the eyebrows raise and so on. These are all very obvious indicators of state of mind.

So it's a good idea to get used to observing people and their reactions - but do it subtly! Politicians and others trained in public speaking make good test subjects for observation. Watch how they stand, what they do with their hands and listen to their speech patterns. Of course, it's easy to tell when they are lying... their lips are moving...

There's just one last thing to mention when it come to awareness, perhaps the most important. We should always consider the role of the Four Pillars in observation.

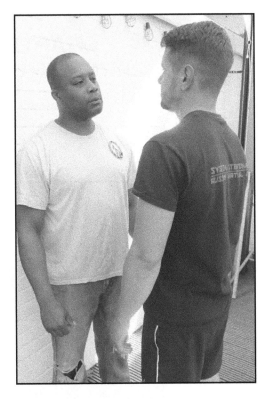

Good posture means we keep the spine straight. Think of the spine as an antennae. When it is in optimum position it can pick up information from all round. If bent or distorted, information gathering is compromised.

Tension, particularly emotional tension, can also affect our ability to process information. It leads us to react with anger, or might mean that we pre-judge people based on prejudice. Breathing is key, as usual, so it's a good idea to take some calming breaths before any observation work.

CHAPTER THREE
PRE - EMPTIVE WORK

The sooner we are aware of a problem, the more options we have in dealing with it. In the previous chapter, we looked at ways of spotting trouble and completely avoiding it. But what if we get caught out? The next stage in the process is working against an attacker pre-emptively. In other words, we take direct action before the person attacks us.

This is where we get into the realm of legalities. I am speaking here from the context of UK law. In terms of background, I worked for a number of years for the Crown Prosecution Service at a London Crown Court. Also, my wife works for the police and one side of my family were, for the most part, coppers. The other side weren't but that's a different story! So I have a good grasp of UK law in general, particularly as it relates to this subject.

You sometimes hear people say "oh, in the UK you are not even allowed to defend yourself!" This is not true. There is no rule in law to say that a person must wait to be struck first before they may defend themselves.

UK self defence law is based around the principle of *reasonable force*. In short, a person may use such force as is reasonable in the circumstances for the purposes of self-defence; defence of another; defence of property; prevention of crime; lawful arrest.

Cases in the UK are tried on an individual basis and, if one were arrested following a confrontation, it would be up to the prosecution to prove that any force used was disproportionate. As a broad example, if a person attacked you with a stick, it would be reasonable to use a stick to defend yourself with. If the attacker drops the stick, tries to escape, or is incapacitated, it would be seen as unreasonable force to keep beating them with your stick.

This is very general, of course, and it depends very much on circumstances. A woman defending herself against a much larger man might extend the range of what is considered reasonable. This is why cases are tried on an individual basis with a jury, so that all circumstances can be taken into account. I'd just stress again that this is UK law. It may well be different where you are, or it may be different if we are from the UK but travelling abroad. Our awareness, then, should also extend to local laws and regulations.

Going back to our pre-emption, it is clear, then, that a person fearing for their own or another's safety can act first. Let's look at some real life examples.

INTENT

I was walking down a wide alleyway at the back of a cinema. One side of the alleyway had a low fence that backed onto gardens at the rear of some houses. Two guys were at the other end of the alleyway, they were looking over the fence into a garden. My first

backed away, and nodded at me, saying "Alright?" or something. I didn't reply, just walked through them and carried on. Round the corner, I called the police to let them know there were a couple of dodgy characters hanging round.

I don't know if they would have done anything or tried to rob me. But I genuinely think that what thought was that they were casing the place, perhaps with an eye to burglary, that was my distinct impression.

I was projecting at that time, in my look, in my body language, was a real "mess with me and you're getting it" attitude. The way they backed off was interesting. Maybe I just got lucky?

As I walked towards them, they saw me and turned. One stood on each side of the path, both watching me. They were both quite tall, I remember one had a long, leather coat on. Useful for hiding burglary gear, I later thought. I maintained eye contact as I approached. I suppose I could have retreated on back round the long way, perhaps that would have been the more sensible thing to do. But somehow I didn't want to back down to these people.

As I drew closer I thought, "if anything happens, I'm going for the one in the coat first, and I'm going to hit him in the throat." It was strange, I really felt that, more than felt it, I was projecting it. My gaze was fixed on the coat guy, but I was still aware of the other one.

When I got to within range, they both

What we see in this example is that pre-emption manifested in attitude. We spoke before about how we project, what image we put out. In this case, it would appear that the image here was enough to discourage any attempt at violence. Although, as our narrator says, the more sensible thing to do may have been to not walk down the alleyway! Still, sometimes things occur before we've barely had time to think about it and this is where being able to "switch on" quickly becomes an important skill.

I also liked that the narrator let the police know about the pair afterwards - this sort of intelligence is very useful for the police, they will normally either check the situation out straight away or, at the very least, add the information into briefings.

Here's another situation where the response was non-verbal but effective.

PRESENCE

So I'm out driving and I stop to nip into a shop. When I come out, this man has parked his car quite close behind, he's not left much of a gap. I reverse my van, slowly, carefully, but I just touch his front bumper. I mean, literally just touch it. The bloke is straight of his car - it's a flash, shiny red thing, I don't know what make. Anyway, he's shouting and swearing, very agitated, very insulting.

I switched my engine off and opened the van door. Now, I'm a fair size and I stood up, but was still in the van doorway. So now I'm literally looming over him, I spread my arms out and firmly said "What?"

You could see him deflate. He was looking up at me and he calmed down straight away, went quite meek. Then I got out of the van and went to look at the

bumper. Not a mark, not even a smudge. I pointed that out to him and he ummed and arred. I took a photo with my phone, just to be sure I had the evidence in case he tried something on later. That done, I got back in the van and drove off.

Once again, the narrator's body language has played a part in getting through the situation. The use of the "high ground" was interesting here, one of the oldest military principles. Also, it's a primal response for most people to back off when confronted by someone large - not always, of course but enough to make it an option worth considering. You wonder what the car driver would have done if the van man were not so intimidating?

There's also the idea of "high ground" in terms of the rights and wrongs of the situation. The van driver had done something wrong but not wrong enough to merit the actions of the car driver.

There's a saying I've heard, "you can't be wrong and strong." Being in the right, being sure and

confident, can help in a situation. Any doubt we have about or own actions, any attempt to lie or deceive, usually reveals itself in some way. And, of course, it can be a fine line between intimidation and bullying. As with most things, context is key.

PRESENCE DRILLS

How do we develop presence or intention? Is it a natural or nurtured attribute? A little of both, I think. We all know or have seen someone who has presence. They walk in a room and everyone knows. That may be a physical presence, a huge body-builder, say, or it can be more subtle.

I once heard of a guy who brought his teacher over from Indonesia to teach in the UK. He was out walking round town with him and they came across a fight - two men were squaring up, with a crowd around them. The guy's first concern was for his teacher in that situation (despite his

teacher's abilities.) The teacher insisted on stopping though, he joined the crowd and stood silently, watching.

The student said a strange thing happened. Both men preparing to fight looked round at the teacher, and the tension of the situation slowly ebbed away. Everyone drifted off, there was no fight. That is an interesting example and use of presence. Difficult to define, but very real in effect.

That type of presence is usually from people who are experienced in highly stressful situations and are very sure in themselves. Their inner calm is in some way projected out to others. This ties back to our earlier work - if you project anger, fear, aggression, that is likely what you will get back.

But it's no use just pretending - unless you are a very good actor, perhaps! We can work to develop this with a good training partner. I don't mean Robert De Niro *Taxi Driver* stuff and I don't mean acting like a stereotypical "hard man." Here's some drills you can try.

Stand in front of your partner, about six feet away. Without saying anything, work through some different postures - hands behind back, chest out, arms crossed and so on. Also change your facial expression. Your partner gives honest feedback on how each one makes them feel on a gut-level. This is important. On an intellectual level, it's our friend standing in front of us pulling funny faces. So try and overcome that and focus on what each posture makes you feel.

Then try that at different ranges, see if there are any changes. Next, start a fair distance apart and have your partner walk towards you. At a certain point, go into your chosen body posture, again your partner notes feelings.

After that, you can add in verbals as you wish. The use of language is a big subject, in short I would say keep any instructions clear and concise. Generally avoid saying "don't" instead, be positive. Reinforce verbal interaction with body language, they both have to match. A simple *Stop!* with palm upraised can be surprisingly effective. I once saw the manager of a club take control of a situation by stating loudly and firmly, "Now, this is what's going to happen..."

The salient point to remember is to make your body language as natural as possible. The more confident and comfortable you feel, the greater the effect of your body language. Uncertainty may reveal itself in a trembling hand or erratic breathing and will undermine your presence. Likewise, puffing yourself up and shouting and swearing may scare some people but to others it gives off signals of fear. Plus, in that overly emotional state, you are less likely to function efficiently on any level, particularly awareness.

Some equate "loud and obvious" with presence or charisma. My experience has been that the loudest person in the room is often the most insecure. We live in age of exaggerated media figures, where drawing constant attention is the path to success. Yet look at what happens to many of those "celebs," they rarely have a happy life. So, calm confidence is the key, at least for most general self defence situations.

There's a huge amount of information out there on this subject. In short, the more of this work you do, the better and more natural it will become. It's a good idea to force yourself into the spotlight every now and then, be that in a work meeting, a social situation and so on. This will force you to act with a certain amount of presence - again, I can't stress enough, not by being forceful and loud, but by being confident and assertive.

thinking about. There is no magic involved, just an understanding of human psychology.

Intention is largely projected through the eyes, so the first drill is to see if we can "capture" someone with the eyes. Stand normally, looking down at the floor. Your partner walks up to you. When they get within touching distance, suddenly look up and stare directly into their eyes. As before, your partner notes how they feel. Did they stop moving?

Once you can do that, the next step is to extend the range. Have you ever been to a boring function or party? I have, now and then. At some point in the evening I will look over to my wife - she may be on the other side of the room, talking to people. If I look at her for a while, she will turn and catch my glance. With the slightest movement of an eyebrow, I can indicate that I want to leave. Then begins the extraction work, saying goodbye, thanks for a lovely time and so on. That is one example of what I mean about this type of work being very natural and part of our daily activities.

I had the same experience with door work - catching a colleague's eye to indicate, with my own eye movement, a potential troublemaker. No words are required, the

Intent is a subset of presence. We can think of it as willpower in a way, the mental force behind any posture or gesture. Systema is the only art I've trained in that works in an in-depth and practical way on this subject. I trained in other arts that often talked about "projecting martial intention." This usually involved pulling a grim, starey-eyed face along with your posture. There were some other, slightly more subtle aspects, but that was largely it. I've found that in Systema, there are numerous methods for developing these skills. I would highly recommend Mikhail Ryabko's film *Visual Strikes & Control,* available from Toronto HQ.

Of course, this brings us into the realm of no-contact work, derided as a matter of course by some - whether through lack of understanding or just good, old fashioned trolling. Yet we all do this every day without understanding is there. Let's try this in a drill.

The set up is the same is before, except you look at your partner as soon as they being walking in. Consciously catch their gaze. When you do, indicate a direction with your eyes. You may need to add in a physical motion at first, too. Again, your partner needs to be honest in their response and feedback. One issue with these type of drills is that the partner knows what are you trying to achieve and can work to block it out. You can add that in later on, at first we need to establish the principle, so just be natural.

This is an easy one to work into your daily

life. If you find yourself on a collision course with someone on a pavement, rather than do the little dance we usually do, see if you can direct them with your eyes. I guess the oldest example of this is the group of pranksters who stand looking up at a tall building and pointing. A group soon gathers, all looking up, and the pranksters slip away leaving everyone wondering what it is they are looking at.

So, we can use our eyes alongside our body language to stop or re-direct another person. But what happens when things get physical?

INSTINCT
I remember we had been to a gig in Shoreditch, London, and were heading back to the hotel at around 1am. We were slightly lost but I knew the rough direction and although my wife was getting a bit nervous, I was pretty relaxed.

Anyway, the street we were on was very quiet apart from the traffic. As we were walking I spotted a single male coming out of a side street and start walking towards us. Nothing out of the ordinary, but I naturally swapped sides with my wife so he was on my side.

He was walking quite nonchalantly and not really looking at us. But as we came to within a meter he suddenly lurched across in front of my wife. I hadn't been particularly conscious of him until then. But whether it was instinct or the drinks I'd had that night, I gave him a solid double handed shove into

was in place to deal with it. And when he did react to a potential threat, it was on a purely instinctive level, appropriate to the situation.

The next thing to note is that the couple didn't break stride, they kept moving. This took them away from the threat and also ties in with that legal requirement of appropriate force. The threat had been neutralised, no need to stay.

the road followed by an aggressive "f– off son!".

As he staggered to find his feet we hadn't even stopped walking so we'd made five or six metres. As we left he made some comment about wanting to know the time. The thing is, as I thought it over later I kept questioning if I'd done the right thing; maybe I'd just shoved some innocent guy into the road. But overall my feeling was the situation really hadn't felt right and I reacted accordingly. Not a bad instinct to have, trust your gut feelings and don't stop moving.

The first thing here is that the narrator, before there was any indication of potential trouble, had changed position. This highlights our awareness work from earlier on - no fuss, no panic, just a simple change of position. That, to me, is the major pre-emptive aspect of this situation - because when something did happen, the narrator

A person overcome by fear or anger may have stopped and engaged with the attacker further. Who knows what the outcome might have been? Instead, our narrator remained calm enough to simply walk away.

Interestingly, he later also questioned his actions, a sign of a caring person. I agree with his conclusion, he listened to his instincts and allowed himself to react accordingly. So often people deny or ignore their instincts and end up two or three steps behind what is going on. This will be a good place, then to talk about acceptance.

ACCEPTANCE

Look at how people react in a stressful situations. It is common to see behaviour such as covering one's eyes, ears or mouth, turning away, extending hands out in front, and so on. What we might call *blocking behaviour*. It's as though the person is trying to block out what is happening, is almost denying it is there.

I've spoken to people who have described a feeling of disbelief in certain situations, or of detachment from events. *This isn't happening to me!* I've found this quite common in people who have little or no experience of violence. They've had the fortune to grow up in a nice environment. Finding themselves in the middle of a fight is a disorientating experience.

Imagine that you had never learnt to swim and you are suddenly dropped into a choppy sea. Without preparation, you might panic, your Fight, Flight, Freeze response triggered. In the case of unfamiliar violence, people most often go into Freeze - a throwback to a time when a defence against a predator was to keep very still and hope it didn't see you. Unfortunately, if the event is already taking place, freeze is the worst option.

Something else people do is try and stop what is happening, or block it out. This usually take the form of the hands up, palms out position, the universal symbol for STOP. As we saw earlier, using this at the right time might get a result. However, once punches start to fly, no-one is going to stop because you put your hands up.

Another thing to consider is that we are trying to stop an action that has already begun - and as we know, action will always beat reaction. In Systema, rather than reaction we talk about developing response - more about that later. But the first step is to break the freeze cycle and accept what is happening.

Just one other point - acceptance here means that we acknowledge what is happening on a psychological level, not passively let it happen.

CONTACT DRILL

The first step is to get used to contact. Have a partner push you around a bit. They don't have to be hard shoves but should be enough to make you move. Observe how your body reacts, also observe your emotional response and your breathing. Accept that you are being pushed and nothing more.

For the next stage, you begin to manage your response to incoming force. The two basic methods are to resist or to absorb. To resist, you use the structure of your body.

For example, stand with one foot forward, body turned sideways on. Your partner pushes on your shoulder. Apply resistance, without leaning. As your partner is, in effect, pushing down into your base, this should be a strong position. Think of pushing a car, or being in a rugby scrum.

We are accepting the force onto the body but organising out structure in a way that counters it. Of course, you can work the same idea with a pull. Your partner pulls on your wrist and you resist from the feet. Again, try not to lean but sit back a little into your stance, sink the weight. You can add in a little rotation from hip or shoulder to help.

There is a measure of tension in the

back, in controlled steps. Once the force is gone, the steps stop. This is whole body work.

Or, we can work from the point of contact. In this case, as the push on the shoulder comes in, we do not step but relax and softly rotate the shoulder in the direction of the force. The push will be neutralised without us having to take a step. As you get more used to it, have your partner push from more challenging angles, with more force and so on. It doesn't have to be a hand, your partner can push with a stick, a knife and so on, each will bring its own challenges. Where you can, exhale as you move, this will help the body to relax more.

above, but it should be selective tension. You can experiment both with levels of tension and where you apply it. This is very important work as it start to give you control over your own nervous system. In a Freeze state, the muscles tense without control, we lock ourselves in place. Conscious control of this process allows us to relax or reinforce as we need too.

On a practical level, this will feed into any work where we do not wish to be moved from a particular spot. It can also work well against people trying to apply a lock to us.

Next, work to absorb the force. This can be done with the whole body - our partner pushes the shoulder and, keeping good posture, we allow the force to move us

A quick word on what we mean by relax. At first, people are either tense or relaxed, with nothing in-between! I see it as a sliding scale or, from my musical background, the volume control on an amp! If we are at 1 we are super tense. Every muscle, top to toe, is clenched tight - so tight that we cannot move. If we are at 10 we are laying down, as relaxed as we can be. Of course, there are some amps that go to 11....

Be aware, then, that your tension and/relaxation is selective. When being pushed, certain parts need to be relaxed but we should not be allowing the head to flop around, for example. We usually need to keep some measure of integrity in our structure somewhere.

A good exercise to develop this, particularly

when it comes to holding something is this. You hold a stick out in both hands, parallel to the floor. Your partner pushes your body with another stick. You have to absorb the pushes, but your stick should not move. In other words, with body relaxed apply selective tension to your hands / forearms, to lock them in place.

This kind of work has a myriad of uses, from moving through a crowd to taking hits. It's a fundamental exercise, and one we do almost every class. As with most, although it seems primarily a physical exercise, there is a psychological component - because as those pushes increase in intensity, or become slaps and strikes, your ego will be pricked at some point, your nervous system will spike. That is the point at which you dig into the breathing to bring yourself back under control. A further version of the same drill will have one person being slapped with focus pads by two or three partners, for example. Again, the aim is to accept what is happening and learn to manage our response to it.

The next aspect of acceptance is this idea of trying to stop something that is already happening. In some martial arts, this is seen in the way people use hard blocks against a punch. Typically, people get

into a stance opposite each other, A throws the required punch and B blocks it with the forearm, or similar. This is okay for training some things but doesn't really mirror real life - because B knows exactly where and when the punch is coming. But what if I have quick reactions, I hear you ask? Okay, let's test them!

REACTION DRILL
A stands with hands held shoulder width apart in front of their chest. B stands a couple of feet away with hands up ready. B's job is to quickly strike out, tapping A's chest. A's job is to clap the hands together against B's striking hand / arm.

I would be very surprised if anyone manages to catch the striking hand before it makes contact. This is because we are reacting to an action. By the time the brain registers B's strike and reacts, the hand has already touched the chest. A usually catches the arm on the way back. As we said, action beats reaction. Consider, then, someone punching you in the face. If you try

and throw a hand up to block it, you will likely be too late. How we get round this will be explained later on, but the short answer is we either pre-empt a movement coming in or accept that it is coming and move with it. In other words, we have a response rather than a reaction.

The concept of acceptance has deeper implications. Often the first step to dealing with emotional issues, addiction and so on is to accept that we have an issue. However, this is taking us beyond our basic work, though I would ask you to consider other aspects of acceptance. Let's now move on to developing our instinctual response

INSTINCT DRILL
We experience the world through our senses. Everyone knows about the five senses - sight, hearing, taste, smell, and touch. This model is so ingrained in our culture that any additional method of perception is usually called "a sixth sense." However, humans actually possess more than five senses. The count can vary

depending upon how you define the word *sense*. However, we can at least add the following to the list: balance, temperature, pain, proprioception

We might also consider our sense of intuition. This is defined as *the ability to understand something instinctively, without the need for conscious reasoning.*It is quite often referred to as gut instinct, working on a hunch, survival instinct, premonition or perhaps the subconcsious. I doubt there are any of us that have not experienced this at some time - that tingling in the neck when someone is looking at you from behind, for example.

I think of intuition as something of an umbrella term for a wide range of things. Our senses working in such away that we are not really aware of, for example. It may also be a combination of that and previous experience, skill and so on. It might just be good or bad luck! As far as the latter goes, I'm with the old saying *"the more I train, the luckier I get!"* Given, of course, the right type of training.

Detractors may denigrate this as "magic"

or fantasy. It is neither, In fact, many new scientific studies are confirming that the ability to understand something instinctively can not only inform but actually improve our decision making. How, then, do we develop this skill? Again, we go into a lot more depth on this in *Systema Awareness*, but here are some simple drills to help develop and fine tune our "other" senses.

Partner A wears a blindfold. Partner B starts some distance off and walks slowly and quietly towards A. When A "feels" B, they move out of the way and avoid B. This is the basic outline for a number of drills. We can place A in different positions - standing, seated, prone. B can vary their intention - neutral, hostile and so on. B can also use a knife, pointing it at a particular spot on A with the intent to stab.

Some people click into this drill very quickly, for others it takes a little time. The trick is to be quiet inside (breathing) and take note of what your body is telling you. People may feel a slight tingle or tension in the muscle, that is an indicator that you should take notice of.

Posture is important too, of course. Think of the spine as an antenna. When upright, it can transmit and receive all round. When bent or distorted

in some way, signals may be blocked. Likewise, pay attention to your focus. If we are aderanilsied and in tunnel vision mode, we are more likley to ignore or be unaware of the body's warning signals.

Bring what you learn from this drill into your daily life. Take more notice of your body feelings, particualrly in stressful or potentially dangerous situations. Studies have shown how in cases of sexual assault in particular, the person attacked oftensaid "something didn't feel right," but went along with the situation in any case. Social pressures, not wanting to make a fuss, putting it down to "imagination" are all blockers of our deep seated intuition, our gut instinct.

In the last example, the narrator told us that "something didn't feel right" about the apporaching man. Information was already being gathered about the person. Perhaps

it was triggered by his gait, facial expression, his body language and so on. This combines with our previous experience to set up these warning signals. So also get used to observing people. Once you understand tension in yourself, you will see it far more clearly in other people. Then, should we need to "go physical" in a situation, we are prepared physcially and mentally to do so. And that leads us into our more intense pre-emptive work.

HITTING FIRST

"I was walking through the car park of a large supermarket at 3.30 in the afternoon. I'd just finished making a call on my mobile and I heard someone say "give me your f------ phone". I turned to see a young guy approaching. Actually my first reaction was that this was some kind of joke, so I asked "What?"

The robber repeated his demand, more aggressively. It seemed crazy to me, so I laughed and told him to "f----- off". The robber shouted his demand, put his head down and came forward quick. As he did so, his right hand dropped to his waist. Without thinking, I shot a kick to his knee and as he went down, punched him in the face. The guy was now laying on the floor in some discomfort. Next to him lay an opened knife.

People nearby rushed over. I loudly said "did you see that, he had a knife! He was going to stab me". I also began acting shaken up, though, to be honest, I felt quite calm. Within seconds all the people were agreeing, they all said they saw the knife even though most of them were some distance away.

Next, the police arrived. I was told off for "talking to witnesses". The robber was now claiming he was "just mucking about." I repeatedly pointed out the fact the robber had a knife. The robber was taken to hospital, he had some damage to his kneecap and I was arrested.

I had a two week wait while the CPS decided whether to go ahead with the case against me or not. Eventually it came through that no charges would be pressed. I also declined to press charges against the lad. In fact, I saw him again a short while later and had a little chat about why he shouldn't go round robbing people."

My first observation on this incident is that the narrator thought that it wasn't real, it was a joke. After all, broad daylight in a busy supermarket car park is not the stereotypical venue for robbery, we usually think of dark alleyways and the like. The first lesson, then, is that anything can happen anywhere.

Once he knew it was real, the narrator issued what we might call a clear, verbal command! This was ignored and the robber moved in. This is where instinct kicked in (literally) as *without thinking,* the narrator gave two strikes and put the attacker to the floor. He also noticed the hand move to the belt, a sign that a knife may be being deployed.

The important point was that he did not wait for the knife to come out, the robber had clearly verbally and physically expressed violent intent so, as soon as he came in range, he was taken care of.

Then there is the follow up and the way this was handled - being sure there were witnesses to back up what happened and so on. Also, when he saw the attacker again later on, he offered advice rather than look for revenge. Hopefully that advice was heeded. This idea of post-event consequences is something we will look at in a later chapter. For now, let's stick with the actual attack itself and what it shows us. Two things triggered the response here - the movement forward and the hand dropping to belt. This relates to distance and perceived threat. We then get an appropriate and direct response - the kick to the knee. This had the effect of not only stopping the charge, but also of bringing the attacker's head forward, perfect position for the follow up strike.

The situation was over in seconds. This is something that is important to bear in mind. In such a situation, particularly with a knife involved, there is no sparring, no bouncing around, our response needs to be precise and overwhelming. Let's start working some drills.

DISTANCE DRILLS

Think back to our instinct drill. If we are receptive, we can sense a person approach, even without sight. However, generally, we should be able to spot someone moving quickly towards us. We get a feel for that by our walking drills, sometimes called zombie / dalek drills.

A stands in place, B walks towards them. If A doesn't move, B barges them out of the way. What A is doing here is watching not only for the physical distance but also listening to the body. At some point, it should be giving out those warning signals we mentioned before. So A should move when they feel uncomfortable.

We all have zones of comfort around us. In normal situations, we are fine with having family and friends very close to us. In other situations, this would make us feel uncomfortable. Imagine standing at an empty bus stop, and the one person behind you stands within touching distance. It would feel odd, right? Of course, on a crowded tube train we "switch off" our discomfort, as proximity is expected and accepted.

So, in this first drill, A's response to this feeling should be to exhale and move out of the way. The feeling brings tension, the exhale releases it and allows us to move. Once you have the idea, there are numerous variations. Adjust speed and intention. Have more than one walker. Have the walkers extend a fist out in front. Each time you increase the intensity a little for A.

This helps establish our base-line "safety line." Any crossing of that line into our personal space should trigger a response. Where appropriate, we are looking for avoidance. Remember, our primary defence is not to be there. Depending on the situation, that might mean creating distance and escaping. In other cases, we need to evade but stay in range. As usual, we start off slow, with obvious movements.

Repeat the same drill, this time with B throwing a punch. Again, the aim is for A to avoid the punch and close or maintain the distance. If you wish, you may also add some deflection work into this drill.

B throws a slow, straight punch to A's nose. A moves to the side slightly, at the same time bringing both hands up to cover the face. As A moves, they rotate a little. B's fist should make contact with A's hands and be deflected out to the side.

The point here is that A is not trying to block the punch, it has already happened. Instead, they move the target out of the way, but bring the hands up to where the target was. Timed correctly, this gives you a contact point with the punch. Rotation will deflect the punch off. Don't try and push it away, that only helps wind up another punch. Instead, you should imagine brushing the punch away, softly. This has the added advantage of giving B less information about what you are doing and put A in a better position to counter.

As before, increase speed as required but try not to get into a regular rhythm. Also, make sure B's punches are on target, no tracking or deliberate missing!

Just as a brief aside, a good way to get used to fists flying about is through pad work. When you are the pad holder, don't hold them out at arms length, bring them back close to your face (if you trust your partner!). Your partner can work speed punches and you can work on your breathing and fear control.

POSITION DRILLS
As we have already touched upon, avoiding the attack is only one part, we need to move into a good position, too. This has two aspects - we need to make sure our posture is not distorted or stuck in place, and we need to ensure we are in the best place to carry out our next task, be it counter or create distance.

Repeat the dodging drills. This time, I want you to check your posture when you avoid - so stop the drill as you avoid and see how you are standing.

For example, when a strike comes to the face, it is quite common for people to lean back to avoid it. This does the job but leaves us in a vulnerable position that is difficult to move out of. In effect, we put ourselves into a "mini freeze" position. The immediate threat has been neutralised, so the body feels safe again. This is dangerous as, until the attacker is no longer capable of touching us, we are still in danger, and now in a worse posture to deal with it. If you are really struggling with this, try another drill.

A places a stick over their shoulders and drapes elbows over it. This forces them to remain in an upright posture. B now feeds in strikes with hand or stick. A will have to use

position is good enough to deliver a strong blow. After all, I can lean away from a punch and extend out to touch the attacker, but at full reach and leaning back, there will be little power in my hit.

Repeat the above drills but this time, A closes in and places a fist somewhere on B. They then push with the fist. If in the right position, you should be able to move B away quite easily. Take note not only of where on the body you push but also the angle.

For example, if I push on the chest in an upward direction, there is very little effect. However, push down at 45 degrees and my partner is sent back. To change the angle of the punch, move the elbow up or down. Keep a straight line between elbow and fist.

This already gives us one response to an attack - we avoid it and push the person away. That may or may not be enough, but we are not yet working pre-emptively, so let's now look at *when* we strike.

TIMING

In UK law, if we are in fear for our own or another's safety, we can act with appropriate force. Consider our last situation - the robber had stated his intentions and then began an aggressive movement. In this case our narrator was perfectly within his legal rights to do what he did. But the question then is, when do we do it? Is there a line that has to

much more footwork and positioning in order to avoid the strike.

Another tip is that A should be constantly moving, not dodge and stop, dodge and stop. One way to help with this is for A to face two or more attackers, this is good for breaking us out of the habit of focusing just on what is directly in front of us.

The next thing to consider is countering the attack. A is the target again. This time, B swings a stick at them. A has to avoid the stick, but move in and tap B on the shoulder. Next, do the same against punches. You can deflect if necessary, but try to do so only with one hand, the other hand is tapping.

As much as possible, shorten any gap between avoid and tap. Ideally, you do them at the same time. It is best to have a relaxed body for this, then you can often wave one shoulder away out of range, using that wave to roll the other shoulder forward for your counter strike.

Following this, we need to be sure that our

be crossed before we act?

We first think back to our distance drill and that feeling of discomfort. For me, that is the major indicator that I should respond. That may not just be down to distance, there may be verbal threats and body language, too. There may also be a clear indication that the person is about to hit me, so that is where we will start our first drill

SPOTTING TENSION DRILL

Generally speaking, a person about to hit you gives some indicators. Some examples are a clenched fist, a tensed shoulder, an elbow pulled back to "cock" the arm. Watch the eyes, too. A person may look around to see who is about, or sometimes they will look down at the floor before punching.

Other people may bounce on their toes a couple of times, or place one hand to touch you in order to gauge distance. In general, there will likely be some behaviour to indicate the imminent arrival of a punch! For our drill, A stands in front of B, just over arm's length away. B makes some kind of movement - lifts a foot, clenches a fist and so on. As soon as they see this movement, A points at it and goes "Ah!"

Really try and sharpen this up until A is spotting the movement quickly each time. Then, have B make more subtle movements - tense a

shoulder, look away, and so on. A once again points and speaks immediately on spotting.

There are three elements to this drill from A's perspective. First, there is picking up the visual cue from B. Second, this visual cue prompts a physical action - the pointing. We are tying our sense of sight in with the nervous system. Third, is the "Ah" sound. It doesn't matter what you say, the important thing is that it making A exhale. You may even find the exhale comes before the point. That is fine - we are conditioning ourselves to notice, exhale and move. And, in this case, move towards the threat, not away from it.

The next step is for A to make contact with the pointing hand. They move to touch with the palm or fist at some point on B's body. If you want, you can add in the push here, to check position and angle. The aim is for A to touch B the instant they pick up on the tell.

After that, we work in groups of four. A now faces three people. One of them, prearranged without A's knowledge, will make the move. I advise at first you go back to large, obvious movements to give A a chance to tune in to this new situation. Of course, A's field of awareness must now much wider.

As the drill progresses, work into smaller movements, then to A making contact as with the partner drill. Once you've worked through this for a while, you should find yourself becoming much more tuned in to the subtle movements of anyone close to you. Remember, the aim is not to become jumpy, your movement should always be smooth - it can be fast but it should not be hurried, it is a response, not a reaction.

You may also find little things happening in your daily life. You open a cupboard, a tin falls out, you've already caught it. I regularly find that if I drop something with one hand the other has caught it before I'm even aware it's been dropped. This is nothing out of the ordinary, these are our normal, human capabilities. They appear odd because, for most of us, they have been dampened down and suppressed for so long.

Now that we have our distance, timing and positioning sorted, we can being working pre-emptive strikes.

TARGETS

CHEST

If we are going to hit someone first, we need to hit them in such a way that prevents or discourages them from attacking us. It may be that a good shove will achieve that, it may need something more drastic. So let's thinks about targets.

For a good push, we work to the chest. We move the mass of the body back over the hips and the person has to step backwards to keep their balance. If we push hard enough and accelerate them, the feet may not be able to keep up, the person falls.

A push will be made stronger by putting our whole body behind it. Have your partner

cross their arms, stand arm's length away and push them. Repeat, but this time step in and push, drop your weight into it. Basic stuff but it sometimes bears repeating. This goes back to our idea of positioning.

So, A and B face off, B makes the move, A steps in and pushes away. This is a useful method for low-key situations, or to create distance. You can also push an attacker into a hedge,over a low wall, or into another person. Also, if you shorten the push, make it more jarring, you can actually wind a person.

There is an important psychological aspect to consider here, too. When a person is going forward, the brain is in aggressive mode. A sharp jolt backwards can switch the brain off for a second. That gives us time to act, to escape or continue with further work against the person. Aggression thrives on success - this is why I rarely recommend the typical "backing off from an attacker with my hands raised" approach. I don't know what is behind me and all I am doing is giving my attacker confidence. Best to resole the situation ASAP.

Of course, the push doesn't have to be to the chest, you can experiment with other positions. The side of the arm is a good one. You could also think about pushing with hip to hips, a good way of clearing a person out of the way. Step in deep and use the weight of the hips to bump the person aside.

FACE

Let's stick with the open hand and next consider slaps to the face. A good slap can knock someone out, though a slap gone wrong can have the effect of aggravating an already angry person!

The palm has a lot of nerve endings, which aids in handling things, but is relatively insensitive to impact. The face, on the other hand, also has a lot of nerve endings but is very sensitive to impact! Think of it as an information exchange - after all, pain is information transmitted by the nervous system. A heavy slap gives far more information to the face than it does the palm.

There is also a psychological aspect to a slap, which may be reinforced by cultural issues. Even so, if enough information is delivered in a short space of time to the brain, it "overloads" and has to sort this info out or, in heavy cases, re-boot!

and drop the palm into the pad.

It is challenging to work power slaps with a partner but it can be done! Start slow and work up to a point at which your partner calls a halt. There are slapping contests in some parts of the world, I suggest watching them for tips. You can also use protection, of course. We sometimes work with a decent head guard, though a heavy slap can still generate impact into the neck and brain.

We train the position of the slap simply by working from our previous drill and placing the hand on the face. We want as much surface contact as possible onto the cheek. You can try different target areas, but for a general slap the cheek is best. If you go a little higher you will hit the ear, so be careful. A cupping ear strike is an obvious hit in a dangerous situation, just be aware of the damage it can cause.

The head guard is good for testing, or scenario work. B can come in aggressively, A has to position and slap before B has the chance to attack. Please do be aware of the potential risks of head impact, though. One or two heavy hits are enough, we don't want to be repeatedly giving each other head trauma in training.

To train the power of the slap, we use focus pads. Start with a big movement, from a neutral position, swing the hand up and over, hitting on the down stroke. Drop the knees as you hit, adding your weight into the strike. Keep the arm relaxed and heavy, you can add a whipping motion in too for extra impact.

NECK

The neck is a target-rich area. Structurally it is relatively weak and through it we can easily access the nervous, respiratory and blood systems. However, this also makes the neck a potentially dangerous place to hit. So please train with great care, and the more devastating strikes should only be considered in the direst of circumstances.

Also, try the same strike from a hands raised position. In this case the palm starts facing out, twist the hips, rotate the hand

When we discuss any target, we have to consider how effective any strike against it might be. When it comes to the nervous system, ie nerve / pressure points and the like, this is particularly important. There are people who are unresponsive to points, who have a high pain tolerance (which might be due to natural factors, or drugs, etc) and we should also bear in mind that thick clothing may nullify the effect of working against some points.

However, there is one point in the neck that is considered a "ninety percenter," in other words it will work a good 90% of the time. And that is the carotid sinus. There is not space to go into full medical detail here, you can easily research that online. But basically, the CS is a baroreceptor that senses changes in blood pressure. If the blood pressure is high, the CS signals the brain to drop it. This is why it is sometimes massaged for people suffering with tachycarida, or as a diagnostic tool

That is a very basic description, but the upshot is that stimulating the CS in some way, will cause the blood pressure to suddenly drop. In a person with normal blood pressure, this will have the effect of stunning them, or even making them pass out.

The CS can be found by placing two fingers an inch or so under the jaw line, between the windpipe and the Sterneocleido - mastoid muscle. You will feel a strong pulse there. As

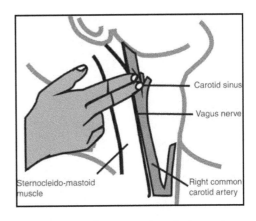

Carotid sinus

Vagus nerve

Sternocleido-mastoid muscle

Right common carotid artery

well as the previous warning, I also ask you to bear this in mind. Some people have CS hypersensitivity, which may be manifested as dizziness at even a light touch. In fact, I have even seen a person in training pass out by tapping the spot themselves. Secondly, repeated striking in this area may dislodge plaque from artery walls, with severe consequences later on. Once again - exercise caution!

As a pre-emptive strike, this is a very effective one that can be set up quite easily. First we train precision, then we train speed. Power is not an issue here, as if the right

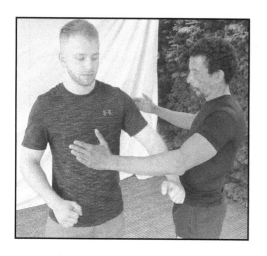

A word here on the concept of "lining up." This applies to all our strikes but especially where we are aiming to hit a specific point. We don't just fling the arm out and hope for the best. Think of as sniper - the shot is lined up before the trigger is pulled. So first think of your "firing arc," this is the area between your outstretched arms. It is easier to hit a target that is within that zone.

spot is hit, very little is needed - and it is generated by the speed and a flick of the hand.

A stands opposite B as in our previous drill. Now, as B begins to move, A reaches out to touch, B's CS. And I mean *touch*. Go slow to start, this is about position and accuracy. To add in the speed, work from the same position but this time A moves fast to slap B on the chest just below the throat, not the point itself.

Second, imagine a line coming out from the centre of your chest. This is what I use as a sight. I line that point up with the target, the CS in this case. If I have a hand on the centre of my chest, all I have to then do is extend it to hit the target. When done properly, it should be unnoticeable to the other person, unless they are particularly aware. Contrast this with having fists raised and clenched, standing square on to them. We are giving signals that allow the other person to prepare, or adjust their own position.

We are hitting with the edge of the hand. The striking hand should be relaxed and you can experiment with flicking it up on impact. So the palm starts facing in, then turns 90 degrees just before impact. This puts the edge of the hand in deep and adds power to the hit.

We can move into this position while talking, with what looks like a relaxed posture. The strike is then thrown out as

required.

The next area of the neck to consider is the muscle that runs down the side of the neck, the sterneomastoid we mentioned earlier. In a blood choke, we apply pressure to each side of the neck at this muscle in order to compress the jugular artery. This cuts off the flow of blood to the brain, and results in unconsciousness. The same can be achieved with a strike into this area. The strike needs to be relaxed and heavy, so it sinks in deep.

This can be done by using the edge of the pad as before, with a hammer fist strike, or by hitting with the forearm. Practice as before - line up your position then reach out with whatever your are striking with to touch the point. This one doesn't have to be quite so pinpoint as we are working into the muscle rather than one spot.

To practice your power, use the forearm to strike into your partner's upper arm. Add in a slight twist again on impact - you should be able to easily knock your partner away, with little apparent effort.

If we look at the

back and front of the neck, we have two targets that are perhaps the most vulnerable parts of the human body - the brainstem and the windpipe. The latter, especially, I would target only in an extreme situation. The brainstem is rarely a pre-emptive target, so we will return to that point later on.

The windpipe, or trachea, is a cartilaginous tube that connects the larynx to the, allowing the passage of air. Any damage can effectively prevent air being drawn into the lungs, so extreme caution is advised when training. Because the windpipe is made of cartilage it is easy to crush - it takes little more effort (physically) than crushing a soft drink can. Once crushed, it cannot be re-opened, requiring a tracheotomy or similar to save life.

The trachea can also be struck, causing it to

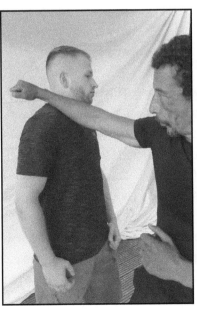 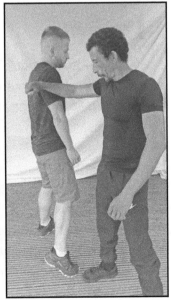

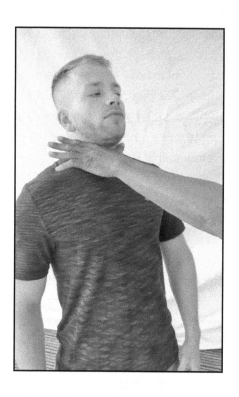

THE HEAD

There are a four points I would target on the head / face for pre-emptive work. The first is a palm strike the centre of the forehead, what some call this the "third eye" area. Simply hit down directly into this area with a heavy palm - the movement is a downward slap that should sink into the target. You may get a knockout from this, you will almost certainly get a knock-back, again giving you time and space.

Dropping down a little, with have a hammer fist to the nose. Similar in terms of positioning to the above, but this time we hammer the fist down onto the nose. The aim is to cause a flinch and move back response. Damaging the nose also has the advantage of brining tears to the eyes and affecting the vision. However, do not rely on breaking a person's nose as a fight-stopper, particularly if they are adrenalised, At the very least, though, it should buy time and space.

swell. In other words, enough power will result in extensive damage. However, even hitting this area lightly will usually cause the person struck to move away, creating space for the defender.

For practice purposes, I would suggest placing your hand lightly on the windpipe and giving a soft push . You can strike with the edge of the hand, as with the CS. You can also try the web strike. This uses the section between thumb and forefinger to hit into the trachea. You can also strike with a punch or the forearm.

Set up as before, with A's strike coming in very lightly to land on the windpipe. To practice power, again you can work on your partner's upper arm.

The third point is the temple. This is another vulnerable area, where four bones of the skull meet. A large artery runs just below these, so any strike here can cause serious damage. However, a lighter hit or slap should result in disorientation and perhaps a knock out.

You can hit here with the base of the fist, with the heel of the palm, or, if closer in, with the elbow. The point to aim for is the small depression at the end of the eyebrows, the

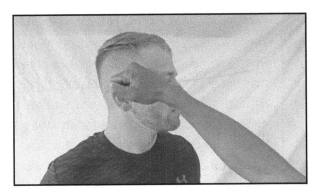

slap them in the groin and then hit the chin. Win, win.

The hook punch should be aimed into the hinge of the jaw, the weakest part of the structure. This is weaker when the mouth is open, so consider asking a question before striking - it creates a distraction and, if answered, your attacker weakens their own structure for you.

spot you massage if you feel a headache coming on. This one is usually quite easy to access, as people tend to think about protecting the jaw rather than here. A good strike comes in from the side on a tight arc and should be a percussive hit.

The last area is the jaw. A sharp blow to the point of the jaw will impact the brain, a hook punch into the side of the jaw may break it. For the first, line up to the person's centreline, then strike up and under the chin. The aim is to sharply jolt the chin back, causing the brain to impact the interior of the skull. You can also kink the brainstem with this move.

Some like to punch for this strike, some like to use the palm heel. Another option is to use the elbow - though this requires a set up.

If you get caught with your hands low, to access the jaw, flick towards the groin with your hand. The person will normally respond by drawing their hips back, bringing the chin forward a little. Now jab your elbow quickly up to strike the chin. Of course, if they don't move, you actually

BODY
Primary target for a pre-emptive body shot is the solar plex. It is a good target if you have been caught out and your hands are down. So we practice the shot from hands up and hands down position.

First, find the spot. Just below the sternum. Your partner should feel it if you push in with your fingers. To access from hands up, consider stroking your chin in a "conversational" stance. From here, drop

joint. When you work the placement, try to keep your body upright and shoulders level. People sometimes give a kick away with a movement of the shoulders. If you find this difficult, have your partner place their hands on your shoulders as you raise a leg. If you rotate correctly from the hip, there will be little or no corresponding movement in the shoulders.

Following this, have your partner walk towards you. Again, place the foot on the knee. If you are a little uncertain about your control, then aim for the thigh just above the knee. At this stage, you can even be a little "flicky" in your work just to build up the accuracy.

The next stage is to push with your foot. Again, we work slow, your partner steps in, place your foot on knee or thigh and push your bodyweight through. Working slow gives you partner time to escape should the

your weight and hammer down into the SP.

If the hand is low, then fire it off from the hip - almost as though you are kicking a football. The punch comes out and up, with the force of the hip behind it.

Both strikes should be short and sharp, sinking in a little for best effect. Be aware that if you deliver a good strike here, the head will likely come forward as the person doubles over.

LEGS

The main target on the legs is the knee. If a person is coming in fast, a kick to the knee will usually stop them at the least, or cause damage as with our earlier event.

First step is to have your partner take a stance in front front you, and simply place your foot on their knee. And I emphasise place, we must take care when working against this weak

knee be locked.

To lock the knee, your kick should land just as the attacker's weight comes into the leg. If a leg is not weighted, any kick may just push it away - that could work as a sweep, perhaps, but not as a strike. So observe how your partner steps, as the heel touches the floor, carefully place your foot on the knee and push a little.

There are two ways to practice power for this kick. The first is to place your foot on your partner's body and push. Again, pay attention to posture. You can work from different angles and your partner can apply differing levels of resistance.

The second way is to kick into a pad or shield or similar. We used to train on an old car tyre in a concrete block (it doubled as a dubious garden ornament.) Aim to kick through the target, not just onto its surface.

If you have worked your pushes correctly, you should find that all power is delivered into the target and none bounces back into the body. If you find yourself going back as you kick, return to the pushes and double check your alignment and levels of tension.

If you want to practice with a little power at faster speeds, I recommend you kick into the thigh above the knee. Even this can be unpleasant at high speed so exercise care. Also be aware that when the lower body is brought to an abrupt halt, the upper body and head will likely still come forward. This helps us line up a second shot, as in our previous event, or move into a control position.

We will describe some specific pre-emptive drills later but, as I'm sure you can see, the process is similar for each target. First work precision, then work power, then work speed. And I stress again that our pre-emptive work should not be "jumpy." It can be worked off of a flinch reaction, but it is better to work through that stage and on to the level of response.

CHAPTER FOUR
FEAR

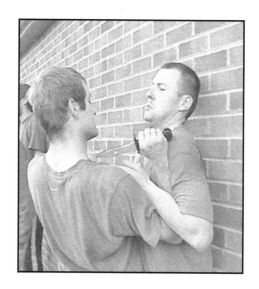

We all know what fear is, have all experienced it and understand its effects. Along with awareness, fear management should be a primary concern in self defence training. Over the years I've seen numerous courses, along the lines of "Learn Self Defence in Six Weeks!" They usually take the form of teaching some basic, gross motor skill techniques, such as a chin jab, hook punch, knee to the groin and so on. All well and good on one level, but there are two missing factors. First is developing the capability to put power into any technique - which is down to all those boring things such as posture, breathing, etc, the things that people on a course don't really want to spend time on.

The second is the concept of fear management. Even in many martial arts, there is little work on fear management, in my experience. To date, Systema has the most in-depth and practical fear management syllabus I've seen, And, as you might expect, breathing is at its heart.

If you are already training in Systema, you will be involved in breath work already. If not, or to study deeper aspects, I point you towards Vladimir Vasiliev's excellent *Let Every Breath* book and other material. What I will do here is talk about the different types of fear we experience, as shown in our examples, and some basic methods to deal with them. Let's start with our first experience.

LOST BOTTLE

There was crowd of us, on Bank Holidays we would go to a seaside town for the weekend. (Bank Holidays are holiday days in the UK, usually a Monday, so giving a long weekend.)

On this occasion, we'd gone to Clacton, a resort on the East Coast. It was usually a weekend of drinking, staying in a cheap B&B, going to local clubs, that sort of thing. I wouldn't say violence was an aim but there were usually some fights involved, either with the locals or with other gangs of lads. It used to be something of an English tradition, starting with the mods and rockers I suppose.

Anyway, half of us had gone down on the Friday afternoon, the rest were coming down later. There were about a dozen of us, we sorted out digs, got something to eat and ended up in a club by the seafront. There were some locals in there and a couple of bouncers in their black suits and dickie bows.

Everything was alright to start, though the locals obviously weren't happy with our presence, especially when one of the lads started to chatting to some girls. After that, you could feel the tension building up, with some words being exchanged. Again, that wasn't really unusual for the time and, to be honest, I didn't think the locals were really going to start anything.

One of the bouncers had other ideas though. I remember, as one record started, he strode into the middle of the dance floor, pulled a small sap out of his jacket and

whacked one of my mates across the face. Blood sprayed everywhere, an obvious broken nose. So then it all kicked off, fists and chairs flying.

But here's the weird thing. I'd been in this situation before, many a time, and never had any problem. This time, though, I dropped my bottle, as we used to say. I ended up squeezed into the corner, trying to get away from the fight. I was gone.

The fight ran its course, we all got out of the club and scattered before the police turned up. I was equal parts annoyed and embarrassed. My mates just laughed. Thing is, we all had it at some time, I suppose, even the toughest. Still, that incident stayed with me and I still remember it above all the more "successful" ones!

I wonder if it was the sudden spray of blood that triggered it? It was quite a spectacular sight. That bouncer was quick, I'll give him that. After that first hit he was laying into anyone near him. He did his job

I suppose, he cleared the club! Anyway, we did see some of the locals later on and hostilities resumed, but that's another story.

Here we see how an unexpected incident caused fear, despite it being a situation the narrator was quite accustomed to. It is interesting how fear has a different effect on different people, and also at different times. It is also interesting how this experience stayed with the person above whatever others they may have had. It is a useful thing, post any situation, to evaluate what happened, to analyse our responses and to take what lesson we can from it. As mentioned, we often do this in class, with people sharing experiences in a non-judgemental environment. We can then extrapolate relevant points and feed them into our work.

In this case, it is difficult to prepare for such an unexpected and primal event. There are, in different types of military training, procedures to get people acclimatised to the sight of blood The same goes for doctors and surgeons, I should imagine. But this type of work would probably seem a little extreme for our everyday, self defence purposes.

Nonetheless, we should be prepared, in any dangerous physical confrontation, for the prospect of injury - ours or another's. It is interesting to speculate that despite so much of our entertainment depicting often extreme violence and its consequences, any appearance of it in the real world will likely to trigger our Freeze, Flight, Fight response, To some extent, we can cover a wide range of situations purely by looking at a managing FFF and the most simple and direct way to do that is through Burst Breathing. Here's two examples.

BURST BREATHING ONE

I was riding my motorbike, going round some nice country lanes. I wasn't driving that fast, it was a sunny day and I was enjoying the view. While you get some nice views on these lanes, and they are quiet, the road surface is not always that good, especially at the edges. There's no kerb and the road often crumbles away at the grass verge.

I was doing around 40-50mph when this car came out of nowhere behind me, some flash sports car. He

screamed past, it felt like inches away, and of course I wobbled, ending up on that crumbly bit of road, in a sort of little gully. There was a grass verge a few inches high on one side, I thought if the front wheel touches that, I'm off. If I steered too hard to get back on the flat tarmac, I might also be off. All I could do was hold a dead straight line down that gully and decelerate, I certainly wasn't going to hit the brakes.

The cool thing was, and bear in mind all this is happening in seconds, was that I went into burst breathing without even thinking about it. Pant, pant, pant... Because of that I didn't panic, I kept the bike steering straight and throttled down.

I came to a halt a bit further down the road and took off my helmet. I continued the breathing as my heart was still pounding a bit. After a couple of minutes I was alright, so resumed my ride. And yes, I did swear at the driver, though he was long gone....

BURST BREATHING TWO

I've been a therapist for around seven years now. My work is mostly people with emotional issues, also dealing with addictions and the like. Every day is different, and it can be challenging but also very rewarding.

I had one client in who, after a number of sessions, began to open up more deeply. This person had suffered considerable trauma and, on this one session in particular, there was a huge release of that trauma. I don't need to go into details but it was a very intense session, as a therapist the most intense I have ever experienced.

At the end, I made sure my client was okay to leave, then sat back down to check who my next client was. Unexpectedly, I suddenly found myself totally over-whelmed by what I had just heard, to be honest I was in floods of tears. I remembered my training. I've breathed my way out if being hit before, so started the same thing now.

I found the breathing gave me

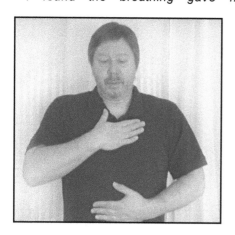

something solid to hang on to. As I went into it I felt as though I was pulling myself out of a deep hole. Once I had regained some measure of composure, I slowed the breathing a little and just sat there. On every exhale, I imagined pushing all the negativity, hurt and pain out. I then got up and moved around a little, rubbed my face, did a little more burst breathing and was then back to normal. Luckily I had a short time until my next appointment, so I took a quick walk outside just to totally clear my head.

That incident really stayed with me. The feeling of sadness hit me like a punch, I felt weak, trembling. Yet it wasn't even my sadness, it was another person's. I learnt a valuable lesson about therapy work, that we have to guard against taking on a clients problems. In fact, when training we were always advised to have our own therapy sessions, too. Personally, I found the Systema breathing really helpful in this situation. It allowed me to stabilise my emotions, gave me some time and space to process what I had just experienced. I now use it as one of the tools to help my clients.

Two quite different examples, then, of how burst breathing can help in a stressful situation. You might think "what has either of these go to do with self defence?" But as I explained at the beginning of the book, self defence, to me, is a broad term, covering all such situations where we find ourselves at risk of physical or psychological harm. You can't hammer fist your way out of every incident, and, importantly, we also see here how we can rid ourselves of considerable stress post-event - something we will return to later on.

BREATHING DRILL

We breathe at different levels, from shallow to belly breathing. Burst, or Recovery, breathing is where we inhale nose and immediately exhale mouth. In other words, a short, sharp, shallow breath - a bit like a dog panting. This is surpassingly effective in calming the nervous system and unlocking any freeze reaction.

To practice it, make sure you are in a comfortable place, inhale and hold your breath. Actually, we get two drills for the price of one here - because a breath hold causes physical and emotional stress.

Hold the breath until the first wave of discomfort. Notice which part of the body is tense, and move it a little to dispel the tension. Also notice any mental tension. Tell your mind to relax - after all, free divers can hold their breath for ten minutes or more, so thirty seconds is not going to hurt us!

When you really have to, release and begin breathing again. Go into Burst Breathing, very short, nose to mouth. As you regain your breath, gradually slow the breathing down until you are on an even keel again.

When winded or short of breath, people often make the mistake of trying to take in a huge lungful of air. Shallow breathing allows us to get at least some oxygen in the body, then use that to begin to stabilise all our systems. Be aware of your posture too, upright spine is best, as any bending will only serve to compress the lungs.

Also be aware of your mental posture. People sometimes like to "hang on" to their pain, or to display it for all to see. Flush it out, every exhale takes some pain or tension away. You may also find some movement helps to, there is a saying "movement is the enemy of fear."

If you want to take this drill up a notch, then take away the control element and have someone else regulate your breathing. To do this, have a partner seal your nose and mouth with their hand. Actually, this drill is best first done without the breather knowing what is going to happen (assuming they are of a level to cope with the resultant stress.) So what we normally do is this.

A is going to practice assisted breath holds. We normally work sitting on the floor. A inhales or exhales and holds. B clamps a hand over A's mouth and nose - this already adds an extra layer of stress.

I tell A to tap when they need to breathe. I tell B not to release their grip on the first tap. Maybe not even the second - this calls for judgement on B's part. In other words, A now has to dig deeper and go beyond what they thought they could do. It works better when unexpected, but you can only do that once!

After a time, you will notice that you begin to BB in any stressful circumstances, as illustrated by our two examples. This really is one of the most profound aspects of Systema training and something I have found useful over and over again.

In the last two incidents, there were no other people directly involved at the time of breathing. But what if there is? What if we are at immediate risk of physical violence? Breathing can still help us, here are two examples.

AUTHORITY

I work for the police as a civilian staff member. At one time my role involved visiting victims of domestic violence to offer support and advice. As I was working on my own, care was taken to ensure that the offending partner was not present when I visited. It was usually the case that they had moved out anyway or, in some cases, the person I was visiting was in a safe home or similar.

On this occasion, however, the perpetrator arrived halfway through the meeting. One thing I was always careful to do was ensure any entrance to the premises was secure. This guy, though, had other ideas. He kicked his way through the back kitchen door and stormed in. He was obviously agitated, possibly under the influence of alcohol.

My first reaction was to get the lady I was visiting away, I told her to go and lock herself in the bathroom. She quickly did so and I was left facing a large, angry man who was shouting and screaming at me. I had my radio on me, but even if I called for back-up I knew it would take some time to arrive. Ideas tumbled through my head, should I run out the front door, should I try and push part him? Should I hit him? None of those really helped, though I found myself backing away from him, hands raised.

Then something happened. I described it afterwards as "having a word with myself" that's how it felt. After all, I was in the right here, I was doing my job, I had a duty of care to the lady and I was in authority. I took a breath, steadied myself, put a palm up and said loudly, "No!"

Not screaming, not agitated, just very firm. That exhale on the No took a lot of the fear out of me and I stepped forward. The man hesitated, I could see doubt in his eyes. I took advantage of his pause to step forward again, saying "Out! Now!"

Perhaps it was surprise at being confronted by a woman (after all he was a bully). Perhaps it was the uniform. Whatever it was, he turned and left, swearing as he went. I immediately called for back up, then sat down and had the shakes. The lady came out and made me a cup of tea, now she was looking after me!

It transpired that he shouldn't have been there at all, according to his bail conditions. So he was later picked up and charged with breaking bail. Without that steadying breath, I don't know what would have happened and the incident did lead to a review of our visiting procedures, so there was a positive outcome overall.

QUICK THINKING

In my younger days, partly through my job, I was involved with some bad types. I was in a certain lifestyle, which included buying drugs. Nothing major, just some weed. But I would buy a big bundle on occasion. At one of those times, I told the dealer I'd drop the money off later. I was a regular, I knew him, so there was no problem with that. However, for whatever reason, I never did go round and pay him. I think part of me was seeing if I could get away with it. It wasn't a huge sum but it was enough to be noticed.

I didn't think any more of it until one evening, I came out of work and had just started walking home. A car pulled up, two guys got out and I was "invited" to get in the back. They sat each of side of me, another guy was driving, the dealer was in the passenger seat.

He had a simple question. "Where's my money?" My heart was pounding, I knew where this could go. I took a second to steady myself with a deep breath and said, "I paid you."

There was little back and forward then, which bought me a little extra time to think. Inspiration! "I gave the money to S-."
She was a mutual friend who lived nearby.

"Well I never got it," came the reply. But I could already see there was some doubt now. I suggested we drive round to her place, so we could sort it out. Now, I didn't want trouble landing on her lap, so when we got there I said, "I'll go and speak to her, we don't want to frighten her with some heavies turning up on her door."

Fortunately, they agreed. I ran up to the door and knocked, S- opened it and I immediately said, "For God's sake, please can you give me £x in cash, right now."

S- was a good friend, she came back with the money and handed it to me, no questions asked. I returned to the car, and handed it over, saying. "She says sorry, she forgot, She's had a lot on lately, family stuff."

The dealer grunted, but he had his money now and I knew he wouldn't do anything to S-. So they drove off and that was that. Of course, I repaid my friend and brought her a nice bottle of wine, too. I think without being able to stay calm and control my breathing, I would have been in serious trouble.

As a positive, that incident caused me to re-think some things in my life and soon after I moved away from that area and those people. So maybe it was meant to happen, maybe it was the warning I needed.

In both these cases, we see how the person was able to stabilise their psyche and operate well under direct threat of physical harm. We also see the dangers of mixing with the wrong type of people and the value of good friends!

Outside of professional circumstances, these situations tend to spring upon us. No-one plans to get threatened! So training for them specifically can be a challenge. I would advise, of course, working through all the various levels of Systema breath work, then integrate that work into various types of pressure testing or scenario drills. We will describe some of these later on.

Remember, our aim is always to balance and calm our psyche in order to build a good response, rather than a flinch-driven fear reaction. The idea of becoming a berserker or putting yourself into a "battle trance" is rarely applicable to everyday self-defence, more to an ancient battlefield. Some also push the "reptile brain" model, where we become little more than a kill-or-be-killed, raging beat, However, the Triune Brain theory from which it is derived has been debunked by scientists.

By all means, we can use visualisation and other methods to bolster our confidence, should we need to, but the heart of any comprehensive fear management system lies in an understanding of the breath-body-mind connection.

It is also worth examining what our fear triggers are. Some of these are universal - falling, restriction, lack of air, pain. Others may be more specific and relate either to previous experiences or phobias. In those cases, Systema work will help bolster any therapy or similar treatments. We will cover falling in the next chapter, but to finish here let's look at some issues around the fear of contact.

We have all flinched at some time, a natural response to the threat of impact. We can learn to use that flinch as part of a reaction or even a response. Without that, though, the flinch is a mini-freeze. Better, if we can, to manage that reaction by taking away some of the fear of contact. Let's start by working from actual contact and pain control.

PAIN CONTROL DRILL

B puts A into a simple lock, a goose-neck, for example. A accepts the lock. B slowly applies pressure and A burst breathes away any pain and tension. As before, B needs to be sensitive, though not too kind! The sharper the pin, the sharper the breath.

Again, we can take this up a notch or two by having two or more people apply locks or pinches to A, even up to four of five people. This is interesting, as A learns how pain in one part of the body can disappear when even more pain appears somewhere else! Again, the main aim is to use BB to manage fear and tension levels and maintain an even psyche.

You can vary this drill in many ways. Rather than a lock, try working on a nerve or pressure point, a light choke, place a hand across the nose and mouth and so on

TAKING STRIKES

Let's expand on our earlier work of taking pushes to the body. The process is the same with strikes. Again, for more detail on all aspects of this work, I refer you to Vladimir's excellent *Strikes* book.

For basic work, though, begin with A on the floor and B pushing into the body with the fist. A first learns to relax, accept the push into the body. This is a great massage method, too.

After this, A can push back with local tension. When done correctly, you will push B away. So, as an example, if B pushes in the abdomen, then A expands the abdomen out, like a balloon inflating, not allowing B's force to come in.

Next, we do the same drill standing. After that, B can start striking lightly. A can work to go soft and absorb, or expand and bounce off the incoming hit.

Be sure to practice all around the body, particularly the face. It's best to absorb strikes here, by allowing the neck to relax and riding the blow. Try moving the crown of your head towards the person hitting you, allowing the jaw to "slip away."

Again, you can increase intensity by having more than one striker, adding in kicks, hitting with pads, slaps and so on.

I don't think I have had one Systema class where no-one has been hit! It is in stark contrast to some other places I have trained, where there was either no contact, or all contact was really heavy, with no management system put in place, usually resulting in injuries. Along with breathing, managing impact should be a daily practice, in some form or other.

RIGHTEOUS ANGER

We will finish the chapter with one more experience. I've mentioned before this idea of "you can't be wrong and strong." So let's look at a situation where what we might call righteous anger overcame fear - with a funny little twist too!

This was when we'd not long moved into our new house. There was a guy over the road who everyone was scared of, he was the neighbourhood bully. He was an older guy, quite big, always had an aggressive air about him. One thing he used to do was take stuff - if he saw it and wanted it, he just took it. People were too afraid of him to say anything.

So one day I was trimming the hedge at the side of the house. I saw this guy come to our front gate and he walked off with our bin. Now, you can get these replaced but you have to pay something, besides this was our bin, what right did he have to take it?

I was that annoyed that I marched over to his place, he was just going in his gate with my bin. I shouted and he turned towards me. It was strange, I didn't feel scared at all, I was so angry that by fear had gone. I guess that showed in my face. Anyway, I went over to him and said, "You stole my bin. I'm taking it back."

He lifted his hands, saying, "Alright, mate, alright. Sorry."

I grabbed the bin and took I back to our garden, still angry. He went indoors. It was only when I got back I realised I still had the shears in my hand, he must have thought I was gong to stab him! We never had any problems with him after that.

Interesting, in this situation, how that anger overcame any fear and how, when a person knows they are in the wrong, they may back down. Of course, that is not always the case, but the addition of a pair of sharp shears and the clear intent of the narrator may have also been a factor!

You might say that, unwittingly as it may have been, our narrator put fear into the other person, to his own advantage. Scaring another person can be one way of gaining the upper hand. However it is a two-edged blade - in some situations you can scare people into desperate measures, you can actually make them a better fighter. It's the old saying about cornering an animal, now it is fighting for survival.

In a situation then, it is usually best, if you are using fear or negotiation, to leave the other person a way out. If someone feels trapped, they may lash out. If they can back out, while still saving some face, they may take that option rather than get physical. There are so many variables, it impossible to offer any hard and fast rules. This is more about feeling and experience, reading a situation and a person's body language.

In general, I would be wary of using threats, instead give the person a positive option. So rather than, "If you don't stop I'm going to smash your face in," try "mate, come on, Do you really want to be getting into all these? We've just come out for a quiet drink, who needs all this aggro?"

In some situations, although they appear aggressive, people do not actually want to fight. It's an ego thing, they feel slighted, or wish to dominate, and if you give them a way to get out without "losing" they will take it.

I've had a couple of situations where I've had to park the ego and be conciliatory, though what I wanted to do was something rather more drastic. We always have to consider consequences, which we will address in a later chapter.

This is a fine line. No-one wants to see a bully getting away with something, or wrong-doing go unpunished. However, we cannot be responsible for everything going wrong in the world and need to recognise that aggression is often a cry for help. If you approach certain situations with that I mind, the solution to resolving it often becomes clearer. As always, use the breathing to regulate your emotional state, ignore the ego, and do what needs to be done to keep everyone safe.

CHAPTER FIVE
TO THE FLOOR

So, then self defence. We need to know how to fight, right? How to wrestle, punch and kick. That's all good On the other hand, how many fights will you get into in your life? If you live in a nice area, the answer will likely be *not many.* However, there is one situation I can guarantee 99% of us will experience at least once on our lives - falling over. And our chances of doing that increase exponentially with age, along with the growing risk of injury.

It makes perfect sense, then, to learn how to fall as part of our self defence. There are many benefits, aside from the obvious. It is great exercise, it helps manage fear of falling, it feeds into ground fighting. There is also a major benefit for training - because the better our partner can fall, the more intense we are able to work. Takedowns and throws can be practiced in a much more dynamic and realistic way when we know our partner can take care of themselves going to the floor.

I teach a wide range of people and I would say, across the board, that falling work is the least popular of all! I sympathise with that, it is something I struggled with a lot when I first began Systema training. I came from a background of strong stances and staying upright, no matter what. Questions such as "what happens if it goes to the ground?" were answered with "don't go to the ground." Suddenly, I was in an environment where there was no stigma attached to falling, in fact it was used as an attack in some cases! Some of the older people I teach have a natural resistance to learning this work, which is a great shame as they will probably need it the most. However, falling work can be practiced in a very controlled and progressive way, to really minimise any fear and discomfort - see *Systema for Seniors* for details on assisted falls.

For our purposes, let's first look at a couple of quite common falling situations, then move into a range of drills for getting to the ground safely.

TRIPS AND FALLS

I was jogging across a park near my house, usual route, I go out a few times a week. I'm not sure if it was something on the ground, or I just tripped over myself but I went over.

But what happened was instead of ploughing into the ground I tucked my head in, went into a perfect falling roll, came to my feet and carried on! I was well pleased with myself! My only regret was it was early in the morning and there wasn't a soul around to see my amazing fall, that was a bit disappointing!

What surprised me most was that I went into the roll totally without thinking, it was just like in training. I was a touch winded but soon got my breath back, the heart rate was up a bit too but I stayed calm throughout - there was more shock from doing something right!

This was when I was out on my bike. During

lockdown I started cycling more to help keep fit. Where I live there's some nice little lanes that are good for cycling, they are usually quiet. Except this day, I went round a bend and there was a van backing into a driveway right in front of me. I slammed on the brakes and swerved, the wheels slid out from under me on the gravel.

Next thing, I'm rolling across the ground, my body just relaxed and I tucked my elbows in. I was straight up before I even really knew what was happening, the van driver was staring at me wide-eyed out of his window. I just nodded, checked the bike and rode on. I had a bit of road-rash, but that was it.

Two experiences that might seem quite minor, almost comical. Yet globally, 684,000 fatal falls occur each year! I have family members who have broken wrists, hips and arms from tripping over a paving slab, slipping on Lino and so on.

In that context, it makes perfect sense to learn how to fall. Let's run through some basic methods, starting from the floor and working up.

FALLING FROM SITTING

We start on the floor in a sitting position and will be falling back. In doing so we will learn some important principles, the first of which is *protect the head*.

When we fall, we do not want he impact to send our head back into the ground. Therefore, if you are falling backwards it is

a good idea to cradle the back of the head in one hand. It may not prevent impact but will at least cushion it. Try and be aware when you go back, of keeping the head forward a little and not letting it loll back.

The second principle is the *sliding hand*. When people fall, the natural response is to put the hands out, perhaps in an attempt to stop the fall. But the fall has already happened and all this usually achieves is damaging the wrist or elbow.

Experienced fallers can work without the hands, but if we do bring a hand out, here's what we should do. When the hand contacts the floor, do not lock it in place, but allow it to slide. This gives us a reference point to the floor, and helps best position the body for impact.

The third principle is *hard floor, soft parts!* We aim to keep bones and joints away from impact and instead land on our more cushiony bits. This usually mean tucking in the arms a little and rounding the body.

To put these principles into practice, we are

going to fall to our right first. From our sitting position, the left hand comes up to protect the back of the head. Take the right hand out to the side as you begin to fall in that direction. As the hand touches the floor, let it slide away from you. This should slow down your fall a little.

Turn into the fall a little so that you are coming down on the side of the body. Avoid landing directly on the spine. As the hand slides, turn your palm up, rotating your arm. This should mean you effectively slide into the impact rather than crash down like a tree being felled. Exhale.

Sit up and try again. You can work the same side or alternate left and right. Practice this until you can do the movement smoothly and without any jarring impact.

FALLING FROM KNEES

Once we can fall from sitting, we go up to the next level, working from the knees. We can fall backwards again from

here, but will also try falling forward. This leads us to another principles, folding the arm.

From a kneeling position, slowly fall forwards and allow one hand to touch the floor. You can practice sliding as before. Say it is the right hand, slide it across to your left which should bring your body down onto its side.

Another method is to fold the arm. You can practice this from a kneeling or push up position. Rotate the hand outwards, so the palm turns up. As you do this, lower the body, rotating the forearm until the weight is in the elbow. Then rotate the elbow in to bring the shoulder to the floor. Once the shoulder touches the floor, roll to the side, and from there onto your back.

Again, we are aiming for a controlled descent rather than a straight fall. Exhale! Practice from the static position then, when you are ready, from the fall.

From kneeling, allow the body to fall forward. Place one hand out, as it contacts the ground, fold as above or slide as before. This should bring you smoothly down onto the shoulder. Don't worry if it's a bit bumpy at first, it takes a little practice.

FALLING FROM THE SQUAT
The next stage is to practice falling from the squat. We will fall backwards - remember the option of protecting the head with one hand.

From a squat, allow the body to fall back. As you go, turn to one side a little so that you are not falling directly onto the back. Extend the hand on that side and allow it to touch the floor.

As it touches, slide, exhale and bring the body down as slowly as you can, onto your side. From there, you can roll onto your back, onto your front, then work back up into a squat and repeat.

FALLING FROM STANDING
Going to ground from standing may seem daunting until you think back to the earlier stages. If I can fall from sitting, all I have to do is sit, then fall! The aim then, is to control our descent down into one of our lower stages, then fall from there. Sounds easy!

To fall back then, we can work from standing into a squat and proceed as before. Simply stand, drop into the squat and fall.

We can also work by the "sitting" method. For this, we extend one leg out in front of us as we lower down. A little more leg stability is required for this one, in effect we are working a pistol squat, though not holding the position. So it might be good to practice this one with some support at first, from an object or other person. Cup the head and take one foot out in front. Move down as though sitting on a chair and, once at the right height go into your rear fall.

Another way to work gradually, is to make ourselves fall by adjusting our stance. To do this, stand, then take one foot out as far as you can - and then a bit further! This will have the effect of giving you a slow fall, but

you will also be lower to the ground. Of course, you can easily modify this to fall backwards or sideways too. This is a good method as, to some extent, it replicates a slip, where one foot slides out and away from us.

If you are feeling brave, you can practice it directly that way too, especially on a slippery surface. Allow one foot to slide away, or you might even use a tennis ball or similar to get the same effect - just remember to be careful.

An option for the forward fall is to bend at the waist, bringing the hands as close as you can to the floor before falling. Again, the lead hand should fold or slide and try to take the feet back as far as you can, this will create the space for you to fall into.

The final method, for now, is to fall to the side from standing. To work this, cross one foot back behind the other and allow the body to drop sideways.
Try to go down rather than too far sideways, in effect going into a squat / sitting position. Extend the arm and allow it to slide out, bringing you down onto your side. From there you can roll onto your back as before.

There is more advanced work we can practice for falling, however, if you have never done any falling before, the exercises here will give you a good method for any potential falls around the home. I would just stress again the importance of taking everything slowly and carefully and working in a safe environment.

ON THE GROUND
I was in a club with a few friends. It was a bit of a rough place and for some reason I can't remember now, I got into a bit of an argument with this other guy. Nothing really happened and I forgot about it. We left the club later and I said "see you" to my friends as they were walking the other way to me.

I was walking on my own and suddenly the guy from the club appears with some of his friends. He starts shouting at me, then comes in and grabs. I grab him back and throw him down, but he still has hold of me and I go to the floor with him.

His friends take this opportunity to close in and start kicking me. Me and the first guy still had hold of each other, so I pulled him on top of me as a bit of a shield. That was okay at first, then he managed to break free and get up.

My friends heard all the shouting and came running back. I don't remember too much what exactly happened, but later they were laughing. They said it looked funny as these guys were coming in to kick me and were falling over. I was kind of grabbing their legs as they kicked, or tripping them with my feet. It was strange, I didn't feel any pressure at all, it was just like being in class.

Anyway, my friends drove the other group off and that was it. Next day I had one bruise on my back, that was it, so the training definitely paid off for me.

We've already spoken about awareness and thinking ahead, so we won't cover that here again, save to say perhaps the narrator could have been more careful coming out of the club and leaving on his own. If you've had an argument with someone, particularly if alcohol is involved, it is not uncommon for them to want to get some payback outside.

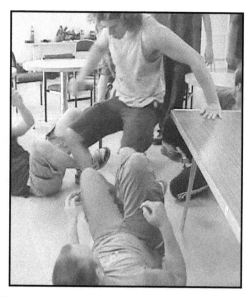

The main factor for me in this incident is going to the ground. The narrator managed to put his attacker on the floor, but unfortunately went with him. This is something we need to be prepared for. On the one hand, we should practice takedowns in such as way that it is difficult for the other person to keep hold of us - more on that later on.

Having said that, even the most skilled can get caught out, let alone slip or trip during a fight. That takes us back to our falling work, this time with the addition of a partner.

For now, I want to concentrate on what happened on the floor. The narrator did a good thing at first, using the person with him as a shield. It doesn't have to be a person, it might be a chair, a table, anything that will give you as bit of cover. Be aware, though, that the cover may be temporary - furniture can be pulled away, people can get up!

The next thing is how the narrator dealt with the kicks. In some ways, when we are on the floor and attackers are standing, we are in quite a strong position. We don't have to worry about balance, and our attacker's legs are vulnerable. Of course, the danger is that we get overwhelmed, in which case we become very vulnerable, to the point of serious injury or worse.

A few years back I heard a prominent combatives instructor advise that the best thing to do in this situation is to go into a foetal position - in other words, curl up and put your hands over your head. This is one of the single most worst pieces of advise I have ever heard. There may be a situation where it is appropriate but it's hard to picture one.

The key to survival on the ground is movement. A static target is an easy target. There is also a psychological issue. In foetal position, you are no longer a person, you are just an object to be kicked. You would be surprised how many people with take a kick if they think that can get away with it. One of our students told of a time he took a young lady out on a first date. A fight broke out in the bar they were in and a man went down to the floor, curled up in a ball. To our friend's horror the young lady took the opportunity to give the poor man on the floor a hefty kick! Needless to say, there was no second date...

This highlights the fact that a person in a ball can literally become a ball. Instead, we need to have an active response to those attacking us. The first step is getting used to moving on the ground

SOLO GROUND MOVEMENT DRILLS
Lay on your back. Start to moving using just one part of the body - for example, you might push yourself along with your feet, or move by rotating the shoulders. Run through as many body areas as you can. Repeat the same on your front. Move using only hands, legs and so on. You can also try moving by using a body wave - raise the chest, push forward from the hips and wave the spine. Also repeat on your sides.

At first, practice this on a smooth floor. Once you are comfortable, work on different surfaces - concrete, grass, gravel, etc. The next step is to work with obstacles. Think about your options. With any object you might go under, over, through, or round. Place some items in your training area -

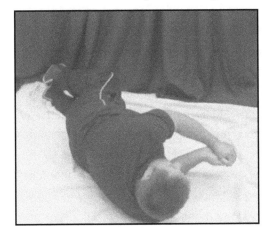

least minimise any impact.

PARTNER GROUND MOVEMENT DRILLS

Once you can move well on your own, it's time to add in more pressure. We repeat our first movement drills, however this time with a partner laying across us. So your partner might lay across your legs or chest and simply acts as a dead weight. Repeat in all the positions as before. You could also try with two partners laying on you for an extra challenge.

For the next drill, have a partner lay across you again. This time, your job is to escape from under them. At first, just use movement and have your partner be a dead weight. Our earlier solo work feeds into this nicely. Assume we have a person laying across your chest. The body is pinned and largely immobile. However, we can use the legs to move. If we raise one knee, say, and thread the other foot through it, we can roll to the side and escape.

chairs, tables, benches and so on. Using the earlier movement patters, find ways to negotiate these obstacles. Try with and without using your hands - you may be carrying something. Also try navigating stairs. For extra sensitivity, try the same drill blindfolded.

This type of work has several benefits. Aside from the practical application - which might be useful in many types of emergency situation as well as a fight - ground movement does a lot to soften the body, strengthen the core and take away much of the fear of being on the ground. Check your Pillars throughout, particularly the breathing, which is key to this exercise. If you find yourself getting stuck, check that you are not holding your breath. Let go of any excess tension and explore the full range of motion of your joints. Try to keep any bony areas away from the floor, or at

From there, explore how you can, for example, pull your partners wrist to help shift their weight. Combine the pull with your movement. Try and work from your strongest position. So rather than lifting a person with just your hands, work by lifting your hips.

As you progress, your partner can apply more and more resistance. We don't want to get too much into ground fighting at this stage, remember this is mostly about ground mobility. But still, as your partner moves to resist, see how you can use that movement to help. See what points of support they use to maintain their position on you and look to remove them.

For example, if your partner is kneeling on you, push the knee out to take away their support. As their weight comes down on you, immediately roll - it is easier to work with a body in motion than one set in place.

Also, think about how you can use clothing in this situation. Grabbing a coat and pulling on it increases your leverage, for example. You can even use your feet for this , with a little practice. Of course, you can get into all sorts of choke work with clothing, as described in *Systema Locks, Holds and Throws*. However, even just for movement drills, grabbing clothes is useful.

You can turn all of these methods into a back and forth flow drill. One person escapes, then immediately takes the dominant position. To switch the drill around, we next try to keep the person on top in place. In other words, we learn how to use them as a shield. From the same set up, the person on top now tries to escape from the person underneath. Again, start slow and gradually build up intensity. The real challenge here is learning to control the person without getting too "locked in" yourself. In a one-on-one situation this is not so bad, but in a situation such as our last example, you want to keep as much freedom of movement as you can - or, at least, view the shield as a temporary measure.

One thing to bear in mind, is learning to be mobile on the floor without using the hands too much. Anytime a hand is placed on the floor, both it and the arm become vulnerable. Besides which, our hands are for attacking! Here's a good drill for that.

Partner A is on the floor. Partner B simply walks towards them. A's job is to avoid contact with the walker, bearing in mind the advise about keeping the hands up. You can increase the intensity by adding more walkers and increasing speed.

A can avoid with large movement, eg

rolling out of the way. They should also practice avoidance by using small movements, virtually staying on the spot.

If you want to add in an element of fear control, work this drill with a large group. Let's say you have a group of twenty. Put five

on the ground and have the other 15 walk around, or have them spar each other. It is up to the five on the floor to protect themselves through movement.

WORKING AGAINST KICKS

Let's move onto the next area, actively working against attacks. We start with A prone on the floor. B steps on different parts of A's body, with a decent amount of pressure. A's job is to escape from the pressure. So if the foot is on the arm, A simply relaxes and rotates the arm out from under the foot. Work all around the body, with A on front, back and sides.

From here, A sits up. B now pushes A with the foot. A simply accepts the force at first and falls back softly. This starts to get us used to contact with a kick. Next, A absorbs the kick and slides it off with body movement. If the kick comes to the chest, say, then A rolls the shoulder away in order to slide the force away.

We now repeat the same drill, but this time A brings a hand up to the body. If we use the above example, as the kick contacts, A places a hand on the chest. As the shoulder rolls to deflect the kick, A's hand also brushes it aside. It is important to state that the deflection here must still come from the body - the hand is purely a guide and contact point.

From here, A next extends the hand out to make contact with the kick as it comes in - so now we are working pre-contact. Once again, the deflection is from the body, don't ever try and block or deflect a full power kick just with the hand. I saw someone try it once, he ended up with a finger facing the wrong way!

Now that we have deflected a kick, what do we do with it? At first, deflect the kick out and to the side, as far as you can. As the foot goes out, push down a little to "fix it" to the ground. This should have the effect of unbalancing your

partner. A second option is for the deflecting arm to immediately rotate back into a strike. It should be easy to hit the groin or punch into the thigh muscles.

For the next option, we start looking at how to use the feet. Remember, on the ground we have no balance issues, so lifting the feet is not a problem! As A deflects, they lean back a little and use a foot to push low down on B's supporting leg. Just above the ankle works well, or to the knee.

That's some ideas for straight kicks or stamps, what if it is a round kick? A sits as before and B now pushes with a round kick. A allows the kick to push them over. Next, A responds by absorbing the force of the push through a soft body.

Next, B starts to actually kick. A takes the kick up high on the arm, with the elbow out slightly. As the kick contacts, A rotates the arm towards the body, softens the torso and so absorbs the force. Start off gentle,

but once you get this right you can deal with quite strong kicks this way.

If A turns their full body into the kick, this becomes a good take down. Absorb the kick, turn into it and look to place the shin across the chest. A's opposite shoulder rotates towards the kicking knee. Lean into the leg a little and B will fall.

What if the kick is to the head? We aren't going to be absorbing that one, instead we

turn to deflection again. This time B puts in a slow round kick to A's head. The first thing for A is to move the head out of the way, first of all by ducking down a little.

A's hands come up, forming a triangle or "little roof" above the head. Using the simple inclined plane principle, this should deflect the kick safely away. Remember we are not blocking the kick and we always use movement as our primary defence!

Another option here is for A to lean back to protect the head, then use a foot to attack B's supporting leg, or kick up to the groin. As you do this work, you will start to get a feel for how vulnerable a person is when kicking, particularly if you are on the ground.

So far, we have been deflecting with the hands, but we can also deflect with the feet. Go back to our straight kick drills. A sits, B gives a straight kick. This time, A leans back, bringing up the foot to deflect the kick out. One neat thing to do here, is to move the kick out towards your hand, which then takes over the deflection, stretching the

kicker out as before. This is a good principle to get used to, look at all the ways you can "pass" an attack from one limb to another. This then frees the deflecting limb to do something else. There are so many ways of doing this, it is impossible to list them all. Play around with the concept and you will soon get the idea. See how the earlier ground movement fits into this too. Often , a little twist or change of position will open up new opportunities.

We also use the feet for takedowns. To start this work, B stands in place and A is on the ground. A moves around and works against B's legs from different positions. Look at all the ways you can apply pressure. One foot can hook behind an ankle. The other can press the knee back. Or both feet go inside B's ankles, then push out sharply, causing B to fall. Also, try pushing the knee outwards from the inside, it is very weak in this direction.

Once you have the static drill down, B starts walking. You can walk through all of the above, plus foot sweeps. As the person steps in, use your foot to sweep the lead leg away. Timing is essential - you want to sweep the foot just as it is touching down , just as the weight is committed, but the position is weak. Of course, you can also use the hands for both these drills too. Pushing

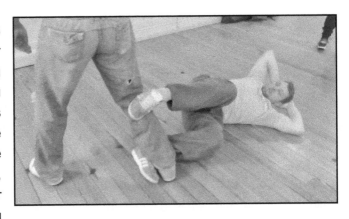

just below the knee on a locked leg will also get a good result.

Another option is to use grabs for takedowns. These can be to trouser legs, to belts, or to hands, if they are in range. For each, be sure to pull the person out of their base of support - not only is it more effective but you won't be pulling the person down on top of you. You can use feet for this work too! Bring both feet up and clasp your partner's wrists between the ankles, it is a surprisingly strong movement if you use the hips.

When working on the floor against kicks, try and be precise in your work. The ankles and knees are both vulnerable to pressure. To test this, press your hand into the side of your partner's weighted ankle. With the correct movement, it is very easy to roll the ankle over and make them stumble.

When doing your drills, don't stress too much about specific techniques, instead look for movements that will bring your hands and feet to these weak spots. By all means increase intensity, but always be sure to exercise control when working against joints. Don't neglect strikes, either, The groin is an obvious target, but punching into muscles to relax them will also destroy structure. Protect your head with movement, and, as much as you can, use all four limbs to counter.

GETTING UP

In any real situation, we generally want to be back up on our feet as quickly as we can, so let's finish with a couple ideas for getting up. The obvious thing is to go on all fours, then stand up from there. However, this brings our hands down and leaves us very open. Instead, it is better to work on getting up without using the hands.

We first bring ourselves up to sitting position - either by a simple sit up or by kicking the legs out. We then place the sole of one foot on top of the other knee, forming a square shape with our legs. This is a good way to sit as we can easily move from this up, down,

or sideways! The next step is to move up onto the knees. Do this by lifting the hands and expanding the chest - imagine this movement lifting your whole body up.

From kneeling position, bring one foot round until its instep is pressed against the other knee. Now push down into that foot and allow the other knee to open out and back. This will bring the body up without having to apply a lot of force with the leg muscles. The rotation of the hip does most of the heavy lifting here rather than tense muscles. Remember to exhale as you lift.

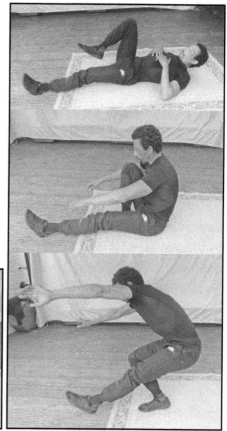

Another option is the cross squat. From your back, lift your legs, then rock forward, crossing your ankles as you do so. Bring your feet under you and you should easily be able to stand up. If you are able, you can do the same using a normal or even by working into a single leg / pistol squat.

If you are in close contact with a person, you may

be able to use them as climbing frame to get yourself up. Grab onto their belt, or whatever you can, and haul yourself up. Be sure to keep the person in tight, and watch for their hands, as yours are being used.

THE MODIFIED SPRAWL

I want to finish this chapter with one other specific way of going to the floor, the modified sprawl. This is a very useful movement to learn and, of course, it can be tweaked in many different ways according to need. We start in standing position. Imagine you are going to perform a burpee, except you only take one foot back. The front leg bends as you bring the hands to the floor. Lower down into the position shown, note how the lead foot is close to the elbow. The forearms rest on the ground.

This posture is not only stable, we can move quickly out of it, whether standing back up,, going completely prone or rolling to the side. It has some defence applications which we will look at later on. But consider also its other uses. If you need to look underneath something, or round a corner. People tend to pick up movement at eye level. Spotting something down at floor height is less easy.

CHAPTER SIX
INTERVENTION

Many of our situations so far have involved a person dealing with direct confrontation of one kind or another. But what about circumstances where the threat is directed to another person? Systema has a significant amount of professional close protection work within its methods. Indeed, in many ways I regard Systema self defence training as *being your own bodyguard.*

We tend to think of bodyguards in terms of celebrities or moves. In fact, if we have kids especially, we are bodyguards all the time. When you take your kids for a walk in the park, you are constantly watching out for them. Threat can come from a dog, a cyclist, a bad person - you are body guarding them!

It doesn't take much to switch this awareness into other aspects of life. As we mentioned before, even a casual scanning of a room as you enter it is a CP method that wen use all the time. Basic awareness of our surroundings and the people in it helps head off a lot of potential problems. But what if we see another person in distress? How can we help? Our next situations feature just that, followed by some drills we can work to develop our skills in this area.

HIDDEN KNIFE

I came out of a club for a smoke and saw that my friend was involved in an argument. There was a lad up in his face, shouting and swearing. This lad had his back to me, my friend was facing me, though was so intent on the man in front of him he didn't really notice me.

My friend had his hands up, trying to calm things down but it wasn't working. Then, from my position, I saw the lad pull a knife from his belt behind his back. It wasn't a big knife, it was what in the UK we call a Stanley knife - like a box cutter, a small blade but razor sharp. Thugs liked using them to slash someone's face, or they'd stab them in the bum.

Anyway, as soon as I saw the knife I acted. The lad was holding it behind his back, getting ready to slash, I reckoned. I ran over, put one arm round his neck, grabbed his wrist with the other and pulled him backwards, off balance. I shouted to my friend "he's got a knife!"

The lad struggled a bit but I had him in a good grip. I made sure to keep him moving backwards and stretched out his arm so I had his elbow against my body. A bit of applied leverage and he dropped the knife. He had some friends with him but they didn't seem keen to get involved and by this time the door staff had seen what was going on and took over. They ejected the lad from the club and his friends went with him. I was right, my friend hadn't seen the knife at all and would have been totally unprepared for a slash. I suppose at lease he had his hands up, so would have taken it across the arms, still, it could have been very dangerous.

THE HECKLER

My band were playing at a music club in Leamington Spa. It was a nice venue with a good crowd, we'd played there a couple of times before with no problems. This time, though, we had an issue. Halfway through the first set, this guy stood right in front of the stage and started heckling. He was not a young man, he appeared to be on his own, and he looked worse the wear with drink.

His heckling was not the best I've heard. At the end of the song he'd shout out "You're shit!" or similar. He was clearly annoying the other people in the audience, but this was a nice venue, so no-one was saying anything to him.

Anyway, first set done and we take a break. Then we go back on for the second set and he pops up again. "You can't sing!" "You're rubbish!" All high quality stuff.

Now, normally in these situations, there's three things that can happen. The first is that the singer or front person of the band deals with it. If you go onstage, learning to deal with hecklers is as important as learning your craft! Stand up comedians, singers, they all have to deal with this nonsense. In this case, however, the singer was… well, he was at a loss, he really didn't know how to handle the situation.

The second thing is that the venue security should be monitoring and would deal with the heckler. For some reason, the stage bouncer that night was not around -

he was actually on the door chatting to his colleague.

The third thing you sometimes get is audience intervention. People around the heckler tell him to shut-up, as he is spoiling the show for everyone. That's what happened in the second set and it was actually my wife telling the guy to be quiet!

Now, when she tells me to shut up, I shut up! However, this guy was not having it. He continued to shout, if anything he got worse. My wife was now next to him and told him to be quiet again. He got angry, turned towards her, and that's when I acted. I was at the back of the stage, behind all my gear, but before I knew it I pushed past the signer, was off the stage and grabbing the guy round the throat. Without pause, I pushed him back, the crowd parted, and I took him towards the exit.

About halfway, he realised what was happening and raised his hand to punch me. It was funny, to me this was all happening in slow motion. The fist came up but before he could launch it, the bouncer finally appeared from the door, grabbed him from behind and dragged him out. I let go and his punch hit empty air as he went off. My last sight of him was his angry little face disappearing out the door.

I returned to he stage and got a round of applause, the best of the night! We continued the set. When I spoke to my wife after, she told me that as I came towards the guy she turned and gave him a deadleg, so that definitely helped! We also made sure, when packing the gear away later, that he wasn't hanging round outside, but he'd long gone.

The really interesting thing for me was how people said I'd moved so quick, yet to me it was all happening really slow. Anyway, that was it. I later left that band, in part because of the singer's attitude, not just in that incident but in others too. I've had other situations as a musician but that's the only time I've had to leave the stage to sort it out!

There are a few things to take from this incident, First, waiting for someone else, perhaps an authority, to take control of the situation. In this case, that was primarily the venue security. In their absence, the lead singer of the band. Neither materialised, so our narrator was forced to take action.

In any situation, it is nice to think that someone will be there to help us. We can't rely on this. It may be that the situation has been engineered purposely to catch us alone, it may just be chance or bad luck. So we have to be prepared to step up, if required.

The second thing is that the time for talking was obviously past. The heckler had ignored all reasonable requests to modify his behaviour. Perhaps a lack of direct action even emboldened him. Who knows how far he would have gone - people on stage are vulnerable to missiles, from bottles to sharpened coins, for example.

The third thing is the method used by the narrator. His main concern was not to engage the heckler in a fight but to remove him from the area. Forward pressure to the throat will move most people if applied correctly. It makes sense bio-mechanically and psychologically, and might be better than grappling or wrestling. The assistance from the narrator's wife was also a nice touch - with the heckler's attention diverted she was able to get in a good de-stabilising blow. Sometimes you don't have to be a great fighter for self-defence, you just have to know what to do and when.

The fourth thing is the time distortion. This is by no means uncommon in a stressful situation, things slow down. Naturally, time can slow to a crawl in a boring job or tedious dinner party! We will discuss ways of working this later on.

The final thing is the use of awareness post-event. I've heard accounts of both

musicians and door staff being jumped on the way out. The guard is down, people are just thinking about getting home. So, it pays to be aware throughout, particularly if there has been some prior incident.

INTERVENTION DRILLS

Let's look at some methods of training intervention. The simplest set up is to have partner A confront partner B. This might be a threatening posture, with verbal threat, it may be an actual grab or hold. Partner C's job is to deal with A in an appropriate way.

The first thing to think about is how C approaches. The ideal position is from A's blind side. If they are drunk and aggressive, A's awareness may not be so great, in any case. If approaching from the rear, C can easily apply a choke, go into head control for a takedown, put on an arm lock or sweep, for example.

If appropriate, C can also strike or kick. Before you do, though, think of the purpose of your strike. Is it to destroy structure? Then hit into a tense, supporting muscle.

To stun or knock out? We spoke about some potential targets before. And, whatever you do, always be ready to switch or shift up a gear if required.

C should also be applying full situational awareness, and have an end goal in mind before engaging. Imagine that B is a youngster, or A has friends nearby. C might want to deal with A then leave the scene quickly. In other circumstances, C might want to restrain A until the authorities arrive. As we like to emphasise, C is always working from a response, not a reaction.

Once you have some basic ideas down, you an add in complications, such as A holding a knife to B. In this case, C must be very aware of the position of the blade and ensure it is away from B and secure before working.

Any of us who sees a friend or family member threatened will get an emotional spike, that's only natural. Use it, by all means, but try not to let it cloud your judgment or overall awareness.

SAVING A LIFE

I've had a few different experiences. People sometimes ask me what my "best fight" was and this and that. Well the best thing wasn't a fight at all. All the years of training, being hit and all the rest, were worth it just for this one incident.

There was a mother and her child walking along the street, I was just behind them. The child was about four or five, I guess, and the mother was letting him push the pushchair rather than be sitting in it. We came to a crossing, it was a double crossing.

The green man lit up, and we all crossed the road. At the second crossing though, the kid just stepped straight out into the road, still pushing the push chair. I don't know what happened, I just instantly reached out, grabbed the kid's collar and yanked him back onto the kerb. A car, it was a Mercedes, smashed into the pushchair and knocked it flying down the road.

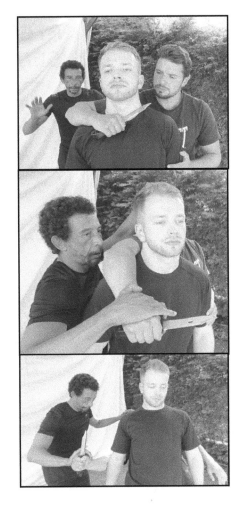

The boy started to cry and I said "I'm sorry about that" to the mother, but she threw her arms around me, saying "Thank you! Thank you!" She even gave me a little kiss on the cheek!

That incident really stuck with me. It showed me that Systema is not always about fighting, or confronting someone. Sometimes those skills and attributes we pick up are not for us, if that makes sense. They are there to help people and put wrong things right. It's about making us a calibrated human being. If you use your skills just for you, that's quite a selfish thing. So that incident really broadened my horizons into doing things out of love, rather than hate.

I have nothing to add to this account, other than it's feedback like this that makes sharing Systema with others so rewarding.

CHAPTER SEVEN
CONSEQUENCES

We have spoken about awareness prior to and during event, to some extent directly after it, too. However, we also need to be aware of the longer term consequences to our actions.

There is an element of conflict in this, After all, our best work tends to be in the moment in Systema, we work on the fly, adapting to the situation as required. How can we do this if we are thinking three weeks ahead? It is a challenge, but if we build this idea into our training, it is one that we can meet. First, however, let's look at some situations featuring consequences ranging from annoying to potentially life changing.

WINDSCREEN

My wife and I had not long moved into a new place. There was a small car park where the residents parked, virtually next door to our place. I'd parked my car there one day and was walking to my house when something caught my eye. It was a group of lads in the corner, doing something shady, maybe a drug deal.

To be honest, I didn't really give them a second glance but one of them must have clocked me looking at them and shouted out to me. I stopped and turned and he just came charging at me. I don't know why, I hadn't said anything, not made any gestures, nothing. Perhaps he felt he had to look tough in front of his mates, perhaps he thought I was someone else, anyway he came charging at me, shouting.

In typical fashion he had his hands out to his sides, chest puffed up, effing and blinding. I let him get just close enough, then popped him on the jaw. I didn't really think too much about it, other than I couldn't really have run off, he was obviously not in the mood for conversation and, to be honest, I'd had a long day ay work!

Anyway, he went to the floor, sat down and had a little think about things. That appeared to be it, his friends showed no sign of helping him. So I backed away and went to my house.

That was it, as far as I was concerned. Obviously not. They'd seen me get out of the car and seen me go into my house. The next morning when I came out, my windscreen had been smashed. I suppose it could have been worse, but now I was really annoyed. I did keep an eye out, but never saw those lads in the car park again, it could be that they weren't even local.

This incident nicely highlights one of the major issues we have to deal with in self defence - follow up aggravation. It was particularly difficult to avoid in this case, the attacker saw the narrator get out of his car and also knew where he lived. In some ways he was lucky it was just the windscreen.

Perhaps the first thing to consider, then, is how much does the other person know about us? Is taking direct action worth the potential

environment for any situation. Are there CCTV cameras? Is someone filming on their phone? Might there be a dashcam? Again, you may be in the right (in which case, as we will see later, CCTV can help.) But it also may help someone ID you and track you down. By the way, I'm not suggesting you do any of this in context of avoiding the law, this is purely working from a self protection perspective.

risk in later kickbacks or escalation? Think about your clothing, or other personal items. Do you have a tattoo of your name on your neck? Are you wearing a highly unusual item of clothing? Is it a good idea to walk around in a Systema t-shirt, for example?

Now widen that out a little - how easy are you to find? Is your house available for all to see on Google Maps? Do you have a strong social media presence? I'm not suggesting you need to be some sort of covert operative in order to avoid potential trouble, just that these are things you should be thinking about anyway as part of your wider self defence training. I know of people who have posted "away on holiday for two weeks!" On social media, then were surprised to find they had been burgled when they returned home.

The next thing to consider is the

From there, be sure that your response is proportional to the situation. In the example above, I feel the narrator was perfectly justified in what he did. Importantly, once the threat had been neutralised, he made no follow up moves, he left the scene. Not that that prevented the later damage in this case! In general, try not to give people a reason to want revenge. There's no need to humiliate people or to create more anger and aggression in them.

Having said that, never say never. There may be a situation where you actively want to discourage any comeback. In which case, reverse the above - let the person know that you know all about them. I was told just this week by one of our guys of an encounter where this was necessary. The aggressor was reminded of the fact that "I know where you live," which successfully de-escalated the situation.

Sometimes, even with the best preparation in the world, we may still find ourselves in a situation such as that car park encounter. Something similar happened to me personally a few years back. One evening I was called out of my house by my neighbour, concerned that something was happening to the elderly gent in the next house along. As it turned out, he had been targeted by a gang of three men, who barged into his house and robbed him. As I came out of my house, they were literally just driving off. He was very shaken as you'd expect, luckily they hadn't physically harmed him. However, it got me to thinking. Would I be prepared to face three robbers, who, as it turns out were "known" to local police, when they have seen me come out of my house?

Quite a dilemma, isn't it? On the one hand I'd feel compelled to try and stop them going in. But if I had come out a little earlier as they were just leaving the house? A likely scenario, presuming I was successful, would be my house being targeted by a group of professional villains, with all that might involve. What would you have done?

The incident in this case was later resolved, with the gang arrested and imprisoned for this and other offences. I had some satisfaction, in that photos I had taken of one of the men (on an earlier "recon" visit) played a small part in the conviction.

So we may have to make a split-second decision with regards to all the above. I think, for most of us, where there is a life in danger, or a vulnerable person is at threat, there would be no hesitation. Likewise, if we are at extreme risk, as the old saying goes, "better to be judged by twelve than carried by six." But if it is our ego or pride that will take the strongest hit? Then a pause for thought may be in order.

But what about if things are the other way round? We feel we have been aggrieved and we are the ones seeking retribution. Can it be justified? That is not for me to answer, as each case will be different. Our next two incidents involve potential and actual revenge, and the following consequences. The first recounts a very serious situation.

REVENGE ONE
A friend dropped round to let me know there was a party going, and did I want to go? It was late and I'd already had a fair bit to drink but I agreed. We ended up at this flat, where I didn't really know anyone and it was all okay until I got into an argument with this guy. Now, like I said, I was quite drunk already so I'm not saying the argument was all his fault. Anyway, I got thrown out of the flat, on my own.

I took offence at this, my friend was still inside, so I started banging on the door. Next thing I know, I have a group of lads around me, and it all kicks off.

I came to with a paramedic helping me. I had no real recollection of what had happened to me. Turns out I had taken a real kicking and my jaw was broken in two places. I was told I must have been hit with something like a wrench or similar. You can imagine the state I was in.

The police got involved and told me if I pressed charges there would be a potential Attempted Murder charge. I turned them down - for various reasons I wasn't interested in police involvement. I did, though, have a real burning for revenge. I was furious, so angry. Of course, I knew it was stupid of me to be so drunk and be acting that way, but still, I could have died!

I went so far as later making some enquiries. It wasn't hard to find out who had been involved, or at least present at the time. At that point though, I had a serious think about the situation. I came to the conclusion that the only way to go "up" from Attempted Murder was actual murder. Was I prepared to do that? Was this really the

way I wanted my life to go?

So, in that sense, this incident prompted a big change in my life. I started to clean up my act, make some changes. Funnily enough, it was about then that I started training in Systema, it seemed to come along at just the right time.

REVENGE TWO

I was a young man, this was at my first job. It involved logging in deliveries, helping to unload vans and lorries, that kind of thing. We had a delivery in one day and for some reason the van driver took against me.

I didn't really know what to say, this was an older man, quite a big guy, shouting insults at me. I tried to keep things calm. What I got back was a torrent of racial abuse that, to be honest, made me want to knock his head off. Still, I kept myself under control and, delivery done, he went on his way.

But I couldn't stop thinking about it, it played on my mind constantly. Why should someone be allowed to get away with that? I wondered if he would ever deliver to my workplace again. Turns out he did, it was part of a local regular route for him.

So a couple of weeks later, I was in my car and I saw him, unloading at another place. I screeched to a halt and jumped out. Without giving him a chance to do anything, I

started laying in to him. Let's just say I left him in no doubt as to the strength of my feelings.

Of course, I was arrested. The police turned up at my house that night, they'd traced me through my registration plate, plus the guy recognised me from where I worked. Long story short, I was likely looking at going away until my boss intervened. He gave me a great character reference and explained something about the situation. Given that, and the fact I was of previous good character, the judge decided to be lenient. I got a suspended sentence and managed to keep my job.

Now, I look back and think how foolish I was to risk everything for that bit of revenge. I'm sure there were other ways I could have handled it, but sometimes, especially when you are young, your anger gets the better of you.

Two incidents, then, where revenge had potentially life-altering consequences. The

first also illustrates, as the narrator clearly describes, the dangers of being drunk and aggressive around people you don't know - particularly in that type of party situation. It also illustrates how an incident that really called for nothing more than a timely intervention or slap, suddenly escalated into a life-threatening assault. On the other hand, it did trigger a drastic change in direction for the person involved, so the long term outcome was positive.

The second incident highlights many of our previous points. Knowledge of the law (the narrator was in the wrong), the legal ramifications of any type of physical action and, fortunately, the intervention of a very considerate employer. Our next incident highlights another major consequence resulting from self defence.

FLATLINE

A group of us were in a pub. We'd never been there before, it was just a place we

went in by chance,

There was a guy in there being really annoying. Very loud, barging his weight around, that kind of thing. Of course, you try and ignore this stuff but he obviously was looking for attention. He started picking on one of our group, insulting him, swearing, getting right up in his face. My friend ignored it until the bully grabbed his shirt. Then my friend hit him in the face and the guy went down, like a sack of spuds.

We didn't want to hang around, so left the place. A day later, my friend got a visit from the police. He was lucky, they said. The guy had hit his head on the fall and was sparked out. An ambulance was called and he actually flatlined on the way to hospital. He was revived and later recovered.

Still, my friend was questioned. What saved him was the barman's statement and also the CCTV from the pub, it had all been filmed. That's how my friend had been traced. So no charges were pressed and that was the end of the situation.

One Punch Syndrome is a serious issue. While exact figures are not available, we know that in the UK dozens of people have died or suffered serious brain trauma over the last ten years as the result of a single punch.

A person is either punched and falls, cracking their head on the floor, or is hit in such a way that causes serious injury. In the case above, thankfully, no permanent damage was done, and there was CCTV evidence that exonerated the puncher. In other cases, people have been jailed, for example there was even one man who punched and killed his friend while "mucking about."

To some extent, we covered this earlier when we spoke about punching to the body rather than the head. Yet even pushing someone over might result in a head injury, so what do we do? I think the best we can do is, again, keep our work proportionate to events and work within the framework of doing the least harm possible. I know some in the combatives world scoff at this idea and propose that we go "all out at all times", smashing our opponents over and over. I'm not saying there's never a need for that, but it makes little sense in the real world to take that as our default position.

Skill levels play a big part here, along with that emotional control we have mentioned several times. The saying goes "if all you have is a hammer, every problem is a nail." If you have a more diverse toolbox, you will find there are many options to resolving a situation beyond punching someone repeatedly in the head.

So, look at how you train, what you are targeting and be aware of what may happen when you hit certain parts of the body. Some, as we have already seen, have dangerous consequences. However, if we can hit the solar plexus and wind a person, that will usually do the trick. If we can collapse a structure and take the person to the floor, in a reasonably controlled way, that will also usually do the trick. In extreme, or escalating situations, we are back to that split second decision

making, which usually comes with time, skill, understanding and experience.

We should always endeavour to be "quiet" in our work. This is where our work is difficult to see, rather than being an overt display of force. In many ways, this work also cuts through resistance - and often, nothing looks like excess force as much as people struggling to apply a very obvious technique without the necessary skill / attribute base.

In terms of training, scenario drills come the closest to replicating the pressure of a real situation. Of course, there are no repercussions from a drill (hopefully!), Nonetheless we can work in elements of decision making into our scenarios that help us understand something about that process under pressure. Before we move on to those, having gone through all our real life incidents, we shall next take a look at some basic physical self defence methods and how to train them.

CHAPTER EIGHT
BASICS

These, then, are our events. We have covered some specific points on each, in this chapter we will examine some other ideas and strategies that may help in these types of situation. As we have already mentioned, our primary attribute is awareness, which gives us the chance to make an informed decision about what actions to take. But anyone can get caught out, or it may be that we have to change course at a certain point.

As the old military saying goes, no plan survives contact with the enemy. However, having no plan to start with is not a good option. Better to have a plan, which can then be adapted on the fly, this is the way military forces work. So we will start with some of the universal elements of any situation and look at ways to manage them.

RANGE

The most important characteristic of any weapon is range. A knife is harmless from 100 yards away. A rifle isn't. A 155mm howitzer may have a range of 20 miles but is useless against someone stood next to it.

Hand-to-hand combat is normally divided in to three ranges - kicking, punching, grappling. This model, while somewhat limited, is good as a starting point. Can my opponent kick me? Are they in range of my punch? So let's first work on judging distance on a visual level.

Partners A and B stand at differing ranges. Start with kicking distance - you can just reach your partner with a kick. One partner moves, the other's task is to maintain the distance. Start slow, you can work up speed as required. Once you have the idea add in some obstacles, work in different environments and so on. This is primarily a visual drill, we observe, orient, decide and act (the *OODA Loop* - more about that later!) The movements are just movements at first, the partner is not particularly trying to do anything, they are just moving around the space, avoiding contact.

The next stage becomes more active. As well as trying to touch with foot or hand, Partner A also now works to increase or decrease the range - meaning that B now has to be more observant and responsive. Think back to our earlier pre-emptive exercises, and bring that knowledge into this drill. Observe and see if you can pick up your partner's movements as early as possible. Does a shoulder lift, or a knee bend? You will quickly learn to accurately predict the coming movement, meaning you can respond rather than react.

This is very important. I often see this type of drill practiced in some places as a "flinch" reaction drill. Everyone is a little hyped up, bouncing on their toes and so on. Fine as a starting point, but we are looking to work through that flinch and into response.

dictated by the stick. Then we go to the more active drill, with one person trying to change the distance. Try to use the eyes less for this one, work more through feel. In fact you can even work it with eyes closed.

After holding the stick, next place the end of the stick on the body. You can rest it on the shoulder at first, then progress to placing it against your chest or similar. We now have to be much more responsive and precise in our work. Again, try and get a much information as you can via the stick. Feel the connection you have with the other person. For added fun, change level and/or add in obstacles as before. Another option is to work in groups of three, you now have to monitor information from two sources!

Transfer this drill to, say, a hostage shooting drill, the kind where targets pop up and you have to shoot if a bad man, or not shoot if it's a hostage. The flinchy shooter will shoot every target - in other words, they react rather than respond.

Bear that image in mind when working this type of drill and, through correct use of breathing, you will learn to respond in a smooth and "intelligent" fashion.

We can also work in a tactile element to this drill. This can be useful in low light situations and starts moving us into the area of instinctive movement. Partners A and B hold a stick between them. The length of the stick is not important. One partner leads the movement, the other has to follow.

At first, each partner holds an end of the stick in their hand and the pair begin moving, just walking around is fine to start. The aim is to maintain the distance, as

TIMING

Once we understand range, we need to work on timing. At what point do we respond? Well, it depends very much on the situation. We have already run through the idea of pre-emption. To be honest, I can think of few situations where we gain any benefit by waiting. If you have to respond, then respond. However, we may get caught out, or we may have to considerably temper our response for some reason.

Partner A moves towards B, from varying distances and directions. At the appropriate point, B has to punch, kick, or grab. Just a single movement is fine, this is about timing more than the strike. As always, start slow and build up speed. Remember to work from different angles and position. This will also teach B to be able to

respond in any direction. It's great having a powerful front kick, but not if the person is to the side of you.

Again, this is primarily a visual drill. You can easily add in elements from the earlier pre-emptive work, targeting and so on. Once you have the idea, A can become more active, they can feed in an attack, or just try and move in fast to touch B. You can also restrict B's options - they can only punch, or grab, or kick, In other words, they have to try and control the range as well as counter.

From here, you can easily work into basic sparring. One partner can only kick, the other can only punch, etc, so there is a constant managing of the range. This will teach you how to control distance and also the timing for launching your attack. Get the timing wrong and you might eat a punch on your way in to grab, for example. Start slow, remember this is a visual drill at first, take the opportunity to observe and learn your partner's body language.

Also, think back to our "flinchy shooter." Don't be the person who, when everyone is working slow, flicks out a quick hit and says "gotcha!" Two points - you are accelerating outside the parameters of the drill. If you are both working fast, that's fine, but work to match speeds..

Also, would your flicky hit actually do anything? We want to be sure that any hits we land have some power behind them. Extending out to full range to get a touch might score a point but have zero impact on your partner. Be sure you are judging range correctly, then, so that when you make contact you have some extension or movement left in the attacking limb.

If you want to test this, slow down a little and use pushes. A feeds in an attack, B moves to counter and places a foot or fist on A. They then push. If you are in the right position, have good angle and placement, you should be able to push your partner away easily. This is a very good drill for learning not only timing but placement and striking angles, so don't neglect it!

POSITION

Having the right range is good, what we also need is position. We might be close enough to hit but facing the wrong way! Our previous drills will work on this in some ways, but here are some more specific ideas for learning where to place your hands and feet. In order to give a nice big, clear movement to work against, we will begin by using the stick.

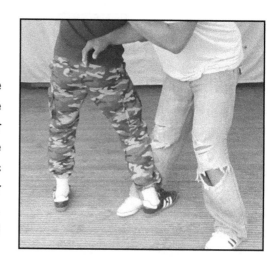

Partner A swings the stick at partner B. At first, it can be a simple, clear movement, reasonably slow. B's job is to evade the stick and, at the same time, move into range, targeting a part of A's body appropriate to the work. We can use this method to work into takedowns, sweeps, strikes and so on, let's examine each in turn. Remember, the aim here is precision - not a flinch, not a move then apply a technique, but to work our counter as we move in. In other words, attack and defence in one movement.

LEGS

We start by attacking the legs. B evades the stick and places their lead knee to A's lead knee. The foot is hooked around A's heel in order to trap the leg in place. In practice, work this carefully. Stop on contact, then B does a slow squat, pushing their knee into A's, who will fall backwards.

Once you have the idea, work in different angles. Try pushing the knee from the side, or the back. You can also pull the supporting foot forward, with the right timing. An important thing to note - when pushing into the knee, don't do it in a straight line. Rotate your knee into the push, it will make your movement much stronger.

This is close range, you can also practice

done these before, we usually incorporate them into our warm-up. For the leg version, raise one foot and, moving from the hip, trace a figure eight with the toes. If you work properly from the hip, you will see how the knee turns in and dips down on the upper part of the movement. This is the part we use to strike.

To develop it, partner A stands close to partner B and pushes with their knee into B's thigh. Again, if you work from the hip, you should be able to move your partner quite easily. Next, put the move in as a light strike - your partner will soon tell you if you are on the right spot! To train more power, have your partner hold a pad or kick shield against their leg. Now you can drop the knee in at full power. It should affect your partner's structure even through the pad. Remember,

work against the knee from kicking range as described in an earlier chapter. Push the foot into the front of the lead knee, or work into the back of the rear knee. Again, take care in your application, the knee is vulnerable when under load. Also work with targeting the rear leg.

Another target that works well at long or close range is the thigh. We aim either for the "dead leg"point on the outside, or the corresponding nerve point on the inside of the thigh. Start by finding each point with your fingers. If a person stands with hands at sides, the outside point is just about where the tip of the middle finger rests. From there, circle round to the same level on the inside of the thigh to find the other point.

The outside point is best hit with an angled strike, and for this we look to our figure eight movement. You may well have

the power comes from hip movement and "dropping" the relaxed leg into the target.

Targeting the inside point works in the same way. Start by placing the knee and pushing. I find an upwards strike works better here. Progress through to the pads as before.

This strike works very well in close, where someone has grabbed, or you are pinned up against a wall, for

example. People often go for the groin in these situations, which can be a good target, of course, if it is available. However most of us are very protective of the groin area and even just the body's flinch reaction works well to protect it. The inner thigh is much more accessible and can be followed up with a groin shot, as it moves the thigh out of the way.

You can target the outer point at kicking range, too. Simply extend the leg out so

that instead of the knee, we are chopping into the thigh with the shin, top of the foot, or even the toes if wearing sturdy footwear. Work through the same procedure as before.

The inside point can be hit with a kick, though you need to be accurate. Again, it is a great way to disrupt the base structure and to open up the target. While we are on that subject, let's just cover something else with kicks. Traditionally, people throw out a kick or punch, withdraw it and kick or punch again. In Systema we aim to make out movements flow, with as little draw-back as possible. If you use the Figure Eight method, you will soon see how one strikes flows into the next. Let's use the above technique as an example.

You knee into the outside of the thigh, which buckles the leg. Instantly rotate the hip and stamp down on the ankle - which is now in a vulnerable position. In other words, you get two strikes from one movement.

You can practice this on the pads. Have your partner hold them at waist height or below, and see how many strikes you can get without bringing the foot back or placing it down. Two or three should be quite easy.

Another way is to work with one or more partners. Have them throw in a slow punch, grab etc, move to avoid it and, again, see how many strikes you can get before putting the foot down. The key - as usual - is relaxation and having good range of motion in the joints.

Once you have the strikes down static, begin adding them in to the earlier movement drills, adjusting speed and intensity as required.

STRIKES

Punching work is covered in great depth in Vladimir Vasiliev's *Strikes* book and various films. So what I will explain here are just a few principles and drills that you can eaisly put into your training. From a self defence perspective, whatever technique we are using we always have to ask, *why am I doing this?*

I have mentioned on many occasions asking martial artists "why do you punch?" The question rarely gets a good answer. Most people say they punch "because we

punch."

My argument is that if you punch (or kick, grab, etc), you should have some idea what you are trying to achieve - a knock out? Wind a person? Shock them? Once you know why you are hitting, you can work with the appropriate method.

In a potentially dangerous situation, you need a punch to be fast and effective. We are not here to spar, or to perform, we need to take control of the situation as quickly and as safely as possible. It is easy then, to say. "well we need to knock the other person out, just keep hitting them in the head until they are unconscious."

You usually see this as a staple of combatives, repeated hammer-first to the

same spot until the person is down.

Okay in some cases but, as we have already mentioned, there are drawbacks - cast your mind back to the chap who flatlined in the ambulance. Think back to our earlier definitions of "appropriate force," not to mention the moral, psychological and other issues that may result.

So while there is often a kind of macho "glamour" attached to going postal on someone who bumped into you, real life is somewhat more nuanced and complicated.

Is it possible, then, to take someone out with a strike safely? Or at least, as safely as possible? There are a couple of methods to consider. We already spoke about targeting the solar plex in a previous chapter. However, any good hit to the torso will affect an attacker's breathing and posture, without the corresponding danger from a knockout, This doesn't mean we

neglect or ignore other types of strike, it all depends on what type of work you want to focus on.

Also, people are very protective of the head, and it is a relatively small and mobile target. If we are in close, the torso is much more accessible. This means working short strikes so that we can effectively hit from grappling range.

We revisit earlier drills to start, to learn placement and angle. Have a partner grab you, place a fist on their body and push. Remember what we said before, don't glance off, push in towards the spine or hips.

But where does the power for the push or strike come from? Typically, we would take a wide stance and push up from the feet. However this is not always practical, plus it leaves the lower body vulnerable. Instead, we use what is called a "floating root" where we don't rely on the stance for power.

There are several ways to develop this, here's one we use a lot. A and B stand opposite each other, fists extended. Your feet should be parallel. Partners touch fists - make sure you have as much contact as possible. A now takes a step back and B leans in, lifting their heels. A supports B's weight fully on their fists.

Be sure to keep good wrist alignment (think

push up position on the floor or against a wall. Bend the arms to get some weight into them, then activate the pecs or shoulders. You should either get a slight lift or feel more support in the hands. The rest of the body remains relaxed.

When applying this in the drill, partner B should feel quite comfortable and confident in the support. Of course, they should also be as relaxed as possible, this will also strengthen the punching structure.

push ups) and the supporting partner should not let their elbows come too far back. Hold the position. If both are comfortable, you can increase the lean. Here's the important part. Remember the feet, they should be parallel, not in a front stance. While keeping the support at the hands, relax the feet, legs and hips. A should be able to lift a foot, circle the hips and so on, without any change in pressure at the fists.

The key to achieving this is in finding another point of support in the upper body. So as A takes the weight of B, they should slightly flex the pecs. This muscle then becomes the base to support for the arms and fists. Or you can try using the shoulders - flex or roll them a little on contact. In other words, we use an internal point of support in the body rather than overly rely on the legs. We establish a line of connection from that support point to the fist. If you have trouble feeling this, get in

After holding for a time, A slowly pushes B away, on an exhale. Then switch roles. Once you can do two hands, work with single fist contact. Monitor your tension levels throughout, shuffle the feet, move the hips - all without changing the feel in the fist.

can practice it by keeping the fist a little relaxed, and almost brushing the skin with your punch.

The muscle punch sinks in a little deeper. If you place your fist on someone's stomach and push in a little you will feel the muscle. So when you hit for this one, the hand should be heavy, let the strike linger a little. The usual aim here is to relax the muscle, particularly useful if you want to collapse structure.

Now we have an idea of floating root, go back to the grab and push drills. Keep your feet close together, avoid using the stance to power the push. Work from that internal support point and see how far you can now push.

But this is still pushing and we need to hit! You can work strikes on a partner, depending on their ability to take them. This is by far the best approach, it gives instant feedback, but it can get unpleasant very quickly! Another option is to hit through a pad placed on the body. On the chest is easiest. Place the fist no more than a foot away, and work your hits. To develop this idea, we also need to know something about depth of strike. This is usually divided into three levels: skin, muscle, organ.

A skin strike is glancing, a surface blow that tends to sting more than anything else. It is good for getting attention, or drawing attention away from somewhere else. You

For organ level, we need to go through the muscle and deep into the body. A typical target might be the liver, for example. Sometimes you can penetrate through the muscle - this usually works if you add some spiral into a muscle punch. Think of a bullet

- it breaks the surface tension, then spirals into the target. To practice this, place the fist, push, then, just as it gets into the muscle, tighten the fist and spiral it.

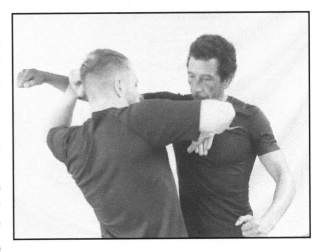

Another option is to bypass the muscle. Imagine the muscles as a suit of armour - where are the gaps that you can slide a dagger into? You can use fingers at first to "prod" into these spaces. Then practice pushing with the fist, then try light but deep strikes, Angle is very important here and with a little work you will soon educate your fists to go to the right spot. This is what Bruce Lee termed "the fist hitting by itself," a very important concept for close-in work.

Naturally, we have to train getting into correct punching range, so go back to those earlier stick drills for the legs and apply them to punching. After working with the stick, have your partner feed in punches or kicks. Of course, if they grab, they bring themselves into range, which actually makes life easier!

As your movement improves, you will find it easier to bypass an attack and get in close enough to strike. However, if you are getting caught out a lot here's another concept you can try - sword and shield. It's quite simple, one arm is the shied, the other the sword. Let's say your attacker throws a punch to your face. You use the left hand to cover and protect as you move in. Remember, the movement is the primary defence, the arm is there to protect, not to try and block the strike.

As you move in, the right hand is the sword, hitting out to strike your attacker. It's a useful thing to picture your strike as a cut or stab from a blade rather than a punch, it tends to help with flow. Remember that kicking work? Apply it to the hands, flow from one strike to the next. If you get stuck, always come back to the figure eight pattern and you will not go far wrong.

Another good way to develop strike flow is the Trinity Strike. This is where we get three hits in one movement. We'll describe one version here, but the main thing is to understand the principle rather than apply it as a set technique.

A stand in front of B, and places a light punch to the solar plex. As B bends a little, A punches up into an uppercut. From here, A

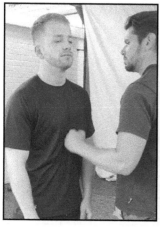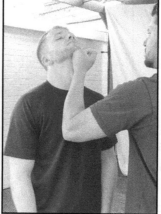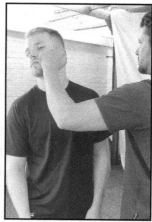

rotates the shoulder back, bringing the fist across the jaw in a hammer strike. The important point is that all power is generated from the shoulder, without withdrawing the fist at any time and without any pause in the movement. Once you have the idea, practice from different angles and start points.

ELBOWS

Where the legs have knees, the arms have elbows! Don't neglect these, they are great striking tools when in close. The elbows are powered by the shoulders, the better shoulder mobility, the more power in your elbow strikes. You can start by pushing, place the elbow against a partner's arm, lift and drop the shoulder forward and push them away.

You can work light elbow strikes to to the body, but be careful not to use the point of the elbow too much. For deeper hits and for training different angles, we go back to

the pads. The pad can be held against the chest, and the elbow strike dropped in, for example. Don't put tension into the strike, just let the arm relax, lift the shoulder to raise the arm, then let it drop, relaxing the knees to sink the bodyweight into the strike.

Another option is to work against two pads. Using either single or both elbows, work your figure eight patterns. Have your partner move the pads around, so you also learn to hit upwards, downwards, etc. See how you can use the movement of chest and shoulders in order to generate power, and keep your movements in close and tight.

To translate this into practical movements, there are some simple drills we can train. The first also shows how an elbow strike can set up a punch.

A stands with one attacker behind, and one in front. The first move is to the rear attacker. This can be a flick to the groin, or an elbow back into the solar plex. This should bring the head forward. A next strikes directly up into the chin. This lifts the hand to punch, which is delivered to the attacker in front. So again, we should be able to get at least three strikes from just one movement.

This is described a set technique but the main thing is to understand the principle. For example, you might lead with the punch to the face. If that misses, bring the elbow back sharply into the head, then rotate the shoulder back for another punch. If you work this concept in slow sparring, you will soon find yourself striking not only with flow but also from all sorts of unusual angles, making this work very difficult to defend against.

As the elbow is primarily a close-range weapon, it is also useful to use against grabs. The key here, is not to fight the grab, particularly if it is against your clothing. All that type of grab does, is tie up the attacker's hand. Leave it there, and strike with the elbow. Then you can escape the grab, or follow up in whatever way is required.

In order to do this, it is important that you remain calm and free when grabbed. Often, people tense and so lock themselves up and restrict their own movement way beyond what the grab is actually doing. A simple drill to work this, is have a partner grab and, first of all, relax yourself. Don't struggle or fight against the grip for now. When you do this, see how much freedom you have in your arms and legs. Can you step? Can you hit or touch your partner? Even if your partner grabs you in a bear hug, if you remain relaxed you will still have a fair amount of movement.

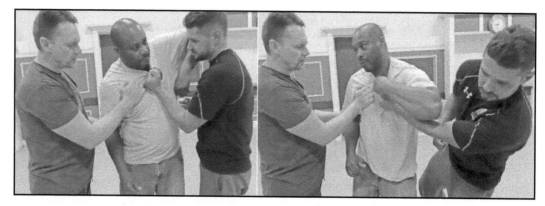

From there, you can start to apply your elbow and knee work. Remember, power is generated by movement, not tension. If you can get some shoulder or hip rotation in, you should be able to deliver a good strike. It will even work against two people, using the principle described earlier - as long as you stay relaxed, which, of course, means breathing!

TAKEDOWNS

One of the best ways to resolve a situation, is to take a person to the floor. This can be done in an number of ways, from soft through to damaging, and gives you time and space to escape or, if required, restrain.

Systema takedowns work primarily on the concept of breaking structure. We all know that an upright spine and level hips and shoulders make the human body able to bear quite heavy loads. Take the spine out of line, even a little, and the strength disappears.

The first step, then, is for partner A to stand, while partner B explores breaking the structure. Start by grabbing a wrist. Think about the three dimensions of any solid object - it has depth, width and height. So we move the wrist in one of those directions, until there is a change in the body. Then we apply a second move, until there is another change, then the third.

Let's say we begin by moving the arm out to the side - width. At some point, A's body will bend a little in the same direction. At that point, B switches to depth and moves the arm back. A will likely also lean a little now. Then B applies height, by moving the arm down towards the floor. It should take very little effort here to make A fall. Experiment in different directions and in the order of movement. You might pull up first, before going to the side and back, for example.

Once you have a feel for working the arm, next work against the torso and head. Now we are going directly against the spine. Place a hand on your partner's forehead.

extra power in your hands, remember, you can add in shoulder /hip rotation and also a weight drop. Exhale as you carry out the movement. This also gives your partner an opportunity to practice falls - win win!

Our goal is to tilt the head back, so forcing the spine to bend. The head is a heavy weight, so where it goes the spine usually follows! Don't just push back in a straight line, though - remember our three dimensions. Rest the palm on the forehead and lightly, rotate a little, lift up, then press back and down. Keep your touch relaxed, their should be no undue tension. Also work slow at first to minimise risk.

Your partner should bend back at some point. However, they can easily re-align by taking a step. So we need to block the hip. Try the same again, this time your other hand is placed on the lower back, slightly to one side. As you move the head, push in a little with the lower hand. Now, push down on the head and your partner should collapse gracefully to the floor. If you need

Once you have this general principle, work from different positions. You can block the hip with your own, for example, or work into the shoulder rather the head. A good method against a punch or grab, is to work against the rear shoulder. Evade the punch and grab the other shoulder from the back, or

push into it from the front. Pull / push back and down, at the same time block the movement of your partner's front leg. You will also find it helps if you squat a little as you apply the move, though try not to lean too much.

You can then begin to put this work into

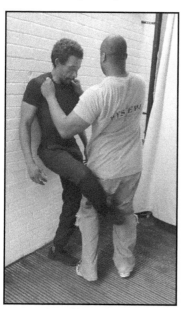

more of a self defence contact. Have your partner grab you and push you up against a wall. You have a big advantage here - not only are both your attacker's hands tied up, you have the support of the wall too, making it easier to use your legs. If in doubt, grab the ears, twist and sink! This kind of work will give you the basics of takedowns, we shall explore further methods later on.

ESCAPING GRABS

Many attacks begin with a grab. In fact, one of the most common forms of street attack in the UK, is a grab with one hand followed by a punch with the other. We need, then, to know how to deal with someone grabbing us. To some extent, we have covered this already with our work on awareness, and controlling distance. However, we may not always have room to evade an attacker.

This takes us back to our idea of range in Systema. Rather than kicking, punching and grappling range, we think of the three ranges as "something is going to happen, something is happening, something has happened." Obviously, by the time we get to being grabbed, something has happened! So let's start there.

The first principle is that being grabbed is not necessarily a bad thing. We know where the

attacker's hand is, and it is tied up to some extent. This contact gives us access into the attacker's systems, whether through using the arm as a lever, or by working into their tension. Our first drill, then, is designed to teach us how to manipulate through a grab.

A grabs B by the shirt / jacket. B remains calm and beings making a figure eight motion with the shoulders. See how this movement affects B. It should move them off balance quite easily. You can amplify the movement by adding in your hips and/or stepping.

Once you have that idea, work from different types of grab. At first, allow your partner to apply the grab fully - in fact the stronger they grip, the better for you. See how you can take their balance with your own movement. Remember our earlier takedown work on depth, width and height. If your partner has grabbed your wrist,

move it in all three dimensions to cause your partner to fall.

The second principle is to understand where the weak points in grabs are. Have your partner grab your wrist. Look at their hand, it is making a C shape. This means that the weakest part of the grip is in that open section. Likewise in a choke - there is not only an opening at the hand end of the arm, there is also space above and below the arm. We use two simple methods to work

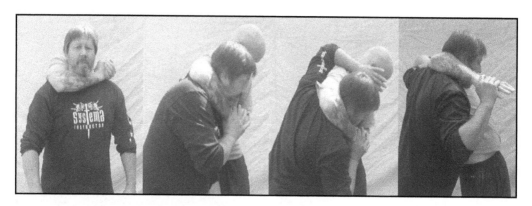

this principle. As before, start with light holds at first and build up resistance. A grabs B's wrist. B relaxes and twists out of the grip working into the gap. Do not struggle, keep the movement smooth. B can work from the arm, or can simply step away to break the grip.

For something more challenging, A places an arm in choke position over B's shoulder. B raises the shoulder which the choking arm is over, and drops the other one. At the same time, turn into the opening at A's hand. You should find yourself facing A, with the choke neutralised.

You can also try turning the opposite way, though this brings you into the strong part of the choke. However, if you first pull the choking elbow down with your hand as you drop the shoulder, you will create a space to escape into. Pull by gripping into the elbow fold, or by grabbing the sleeve. The important thing in each case is the motion of the shoulders and the body turn. Think of the body as pendulum, swing from the hips, do not try and force your way out with strength.

Of course you can work the same against a bear-hug or any other deeper hold. Look at the shape and work towards the space. However, against a strong grip it may also be necessary to add in another principle - working directly against the person.

We can do this with a movement or a strike.

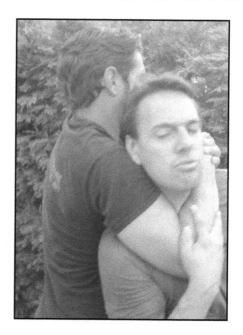

Have your partner apply a bear hug. If we are quick, we may be able to drop into the space below it. But once it is applied, that is difficult. Instead, one foot takes a step back behind your partner's leg. Lean forward slightly as you do this. From there, straighten up sharply, pushing your hip forward into your partner. This should break their structure, sending their body backwards, so breaking the grip. Remember, the power is in the movement, not in tension.

Another way to work direct, is to manipulate the attacker's limb or head. Go back to our earlier choke escape. This time, as you turn into your partner, bring the nearest hand up onto their face. Rotate their head way and down as you twist, so breaking their balance.

The third way to work direct, is to strike. This may be a punch, or you may knee or elbow, even use the head in some cases.

Provided you can keep your structure, you should be able to generate a strong strike even at this range. Target a weak spot, eg ribs, groin, etc. The strike should not be done in isolation, use it to break the attacker's tension, then escape the grip. We have already practiced this, by working a push against a grab. You can also hit, depending on your partner's ability to take strikes.

Consider, also, how you can use other things to help escape. Push your attacker into an object, off a kerb, and so on, anything that will disrupt their balance and help you escape.

Once you have run through each of these methods

slowly, go back and start adding in more speed and intent from your partner. Work simple grabs at first, then up to chokes, bear hugs, etc. Don't lose sight of the fact that the best defence is to avoid the grab entirely, this is just preparation for the worst case scenario.

Explore your range of movements, too. The Modified Sprawl we showed earlier works well against a single or double leg shoot. This example highlights the importance of building good movement patterns in our training. The more adaptable we are, the more options we have when it comes to dealing with grabs and holds.

DUELLING

There is one important concept I would like to mention here before we continue, and that is our general approach to learning and applying our work. In some ways it relates more to our later sparring concepts, but I include it here as it is a good habit to get into as early on as possible in our training. It will help a lot with mindset later on. In

many martial art and action films, fights are often set up as a duel. The hero and villain square off, swap some pithy banter, then begin to fight. At some point during the fight, one person is knocked down and the other one waits for them to get up before continuing.

I hope you can see the drawbacks in this approach from a self defence perspective. Obviously, films are entertainment, but it is interesting to see how much they influence our actions in real life. As we have already established, we have every right, under UK law at least, to act in a pre-emptive fashion if we feel threatened. In other words, we don't have to square off with someone. In fact, I would generally advise against it. At the first hint of trouble, we should be responding. That may be to create distance, it may be to verbally de-escalate, it may be to take direct action.

On no account should we imagine that we are the hero of our own movie. That will draw in the ego and cloud our judgement. If it is appropriate, there is nothing shameful about retreat. I once took a door job for an 18th birthday party. Long story short, I had considerable trouble from one young man, he was very drunk and aggressive. I got him off the premises at the end of the night and the staff locked up. Of course, he was hanging around outside with his pals. When it was time for me to leave, I had two options. Go out the front door and get into a big fight with some drunk teenagers. Or, go out the back door, get in my car and be away home. Guess which one I did? Now, my ego wanted to go out and give him what for. But what would that have achieved? Nothing positive. Better not to be there at all.

DE-ESCALATION

We should also be building this aspect of self defence into our training. It leads into body language, personal communication and so on, another deep area of study. For now, here are some basic tips that you can applying in any confrontation. You can also work these into the scenario drills we describe later on, with a little role playing!

1. DON'T ANTAGONISE

De-escalation means reducing tension between you and the other party. Be calm in your response, avoid insults or inflammatory language. Clearly express your wish to resolve the situation peacefully.

2. DROP YOUR EGO

If you were in the wrong, apologise (also a good opportunity to raise your hands!). If you were in the right, you might still apologise. Let the other person "win," especially in cases where you may end up fighting over nothing.

3. BE FIRM

Giving way doesn't mean surrendering.

Don't appear weak or scared (unless appropriate). In some cases it is better to be authoritative, in other cases that can trigger a bad response.

4. EMPATHY

Establish rapport. Ask the person's name. Tell them, "yeah the same thing happened to me last week." Or make something up, "sorry, I'm rushing to see my gran, she's ill." I heard of a person confronted by some street toughs who was so good at this, he had them in tears by the end. They all shook his hand and went away!

Empathy works both ways. Be aware that aggression is often a mask for fear. It may also be that the other person is going through severe issues. Be sensitive to that.

5. DON'T ATTACH
Another approach is to remain completely impassive and impersonal. This can sometimes confuse people - and confusion is the first step to compliance.

6. OFFER A WAY OUT
In general, I've found that most people don't actually want to fight, but they need to look good in front of their mates, partner, etc. Back them into a corner, or frighten them enough and you can actually make the person a better fighter! Instead, offer a clear way out. That can be physical or psychological. You might step aside to allow them to move away. You might offer a handshake and apologise.

7. INTIMIDATE
In certain situations, you may be able to intimidate the other person into leaving you alone. You might act a little crazy, use eye contact (if you have that ability) and so on. This can be a knife-edge though, so judge its use very carefully. Nothing fails more than a tough guy deflated. It can literally be like watching a balloon slowly going down, complete with the sound...

8. BANTER
I've seen a few situations resolved with a cracking putdown. It can be tricky, but a good line might work well if facing a group - target the big mouth with a putdown and get his mates to laugh at him. You need to have a sharp wit for this, or some lines prepared - just like our earlier comedian knowing how to deal with a heckler.

One of my favourites, from a while back was a flash guy who was "giving it large," he said something about being "the local David Beckham." The man he was fronting shrugged and, deadpan, replied, "you look more like Dave from Peckham." End of argument!

9. CALL FOR HELP
Never be concerned about calling for help. There may be people around who haven't seen what is happening. They may or may not directly intervene, they may, at least, record the aggressors on their phone, or call the police. If going into a dangerous place, have your phone to hand, with the police on

speed dial. Or, it may be you call for help in another way. "Do you know who my brother is," for example. This is a type of intimidation I guess, again it needs to be carefully judged.

10. MISDIRECTION

If you are the object of aggression, can you deflect to another target. "It wasn't me, it was them." Not always fair, perhaps and you may get someone else into trouble - so choose someone who looks like they can handle themselves!

Or you might try distracting attention, with a movement, with a gesture, you can even do it with the eyes. The old "look over the shoulder" trick works surprisingly well. This may either break the aggressor's flow, or give you a chance to create distance. The real experts at this are magicians and pickpockets. Take a look at Apollo Robbins on Youtube, he is a master of managing attention.

11. FIGHTING WITHOUT FIGHTING

I'm sure you've all heard the Bruce Lee quote, based on Sun Tzu. I saw a prime example of this on the door once, a young challenger, determined to take on the Head Doorman. The Doorman offered to take the fight outside. The young man agreed and was ushered through the fire exit, which was then firmly shut behind him. Job done. So you may be able to lead your aggressor out and away, or perhaps to a busier or CCTV covered area where it is difficult for

them to take any action.

There are numerous variables in any situation, but this list will give you some guidelines. Ultimately, we are working against the other person's will to fight. If we remove that, we avoid the need for direct action. However, we must always be prepared for the eventuality, for as long as the person is in the vicinity. Don't get pulled in by the old "turn away, then swing back and punch" trick, for example. Maintain alertness and awareness until you are completely out of the situation.

Also be aware of the other people around, particularly if they might be witnesses later on. If they report that you were screaming at someone before hitting them, it doesn't look good in court. Better to be heard saying "please leave me alone, don't hurt me! " or similar, even as you are hitting someone. Spoken words are quite clear, especially if reported by several people. Physical actions can often be subject to interpretation.

If you do go to court, I would advise against mentioning that you practice martial arts unless you really have to. For some reason it tends to go against you, at least in the UK, especially if you have injured someone.

I would also advise that as soon as it is safe to do so, you write down notes about the event. Contemporaneous notes are counted as strong evidence in UK courts.

CHAPTER NINE
SITUATIONS

Now that we have some basics to work with, let's look at putting them into use in specific situations. These reflect our earlier reported experiences, as well as other potential situations. As before, we aren't looking to provide a list of techniques that cover every single possible eventuality, more an idea of strategies that can be adapted and tuned to suit the situation. We will also include some ideas around using every day items as improvised weapons, plus how to work in confined spaces and other environments.

We will start with something quite common. It is certainly true, in my own experience, that a fight or conflict rarely occurs when there are only two people present. That may be the case with road rage or robbery incidents, or similar, but normally we are in a bar or club, at an event, and so on.

Another aspect of this is that we also may not be on our own, and our partner can assist in any confrontation. We have already looked at some intervention drills, but in Systema we also learn to work as a team. This supposes that you can train with your partner, of course. At the very least, if you have a partner or children who don't have the time or inclination to train, I would advise at least setting out some basic procedures to follow in the event of a situation. This might be as simple as "hold my left hand and don't let go" to "we'll stand back to back," As previously mentioned,

have procedures in place, such as "if we get separated I will meet you at - " A little preparation can go a long way.

We will begin by working against two people, then go to working in a crowd. Mass brawls were part of my teenage landscape and one of the first things that caught my eye about Systema was the mass attack work. It was the first time, in around 20 years of martial arts training, that I had seen real crowd work, as opposed to standing in the middle of a circle of attackers who obligingly wait their turn!

TWO AGAINST ONE

First off, what is the situation? If it is robbery, you may find that the two people have a plan for working together. One may provide a distraction, while the other picks your pocket. Or, as in our earlier bag snatch, one is the driver while the other carries out the robbery.

In this case, we have already spoken about awareness and some ideas to help prevent robbery. We have also covered drills that teach you to control space and distance. These can be put to good use should you feel wary about anyone who approaches you. Of course, you may find you don't always have a lot of room to manoeuvre, but putting your back to a wall can protect your "six" to some extent.

Another important principle when dealing with multiples, is the concept of *shielding*.

around. Use the "handles" such as elbows, hips, etc, to keep your shield in place. Try not to get too deeply into grappling them, as this will give the other partner an opening to attack.

Another possibility is to use a takedown to bring one attacker to the ground in front of you. This time, A and B front up C. One of them then initiates a grab or strike. C has to deal with the attack, then take the attacker down. Be sure to bring them straight down in front of you to act as a barrier to the other person. From this, we can also begin working the principle of joining. Have the second person attack just after the first. Attacker two now has to lean in a little to reach C. This means a quick pull on the arm or upper body will assist the attacker in tripping over their friend. Now C has A and B together, they can either escape or pin one partner to the floor with the other.

This is where you use one person to block the movement of another, in effect you use them as a shield.

This in turn leads to the principle of *stacking*, in other words we position ourselves as much as possible to deal with people one at a time. A further principle from that point is *joining*. If we can attach two or more people together in some way, we can often use one movement to affect both people.

For our first drill, we will have A and B approaching C. The job for C is to not get caught between A and B but always position to have one of them in front of the other. At first, try this with footwork and maintaining distance. Then try closer in. In some ways this is easier, as C can now grab one of the attackers and physically manoeuvre them into place.

Think back to our earlier work on structure breaking and moving people

What if we find ourselves caught between attackers? If they are striking, we can move. If they both grab us, then we need to apply the joining principle. To drill this, A and B grab C's arms. Just a normal grab is fine at first, no fancy lock is necessary, just hold C in place. C now explores just how much movement they have despite the holds. The feet, hips, shoulders, all are free to move to a large extent.

So think first of all how you could, say kick A or B in order to loosen one grip, then deal with the other person. Once you get that idea, you can begin to work with deeper, more complex grips. Have one partner grab round the neck, the other lock an arm, for example.

The procedure is always the same. Relax without breaking structure, see what parts of the body you can move and use them to attack one then the other partner. As an example, if the feet are free, you can step behind one to take them off balance, so freeing an arm to strike the other.

This is good, though a little static, and we are not joining yet. So, repeat the first drill, the arm grab. This time as soon as the grab comes on, C brings one of their hands over the other. Use the shoulders to power the moment, remember we never resist at the point of contact. This should have the effect of bringing A and B close together. See how you can position the arms so that A's arm is over B's. Press down on one and you will find you can take two people down with one movement.

Take a little time to practice this, then start working with deeper grabs and adding in a little movement. You may even find that in this situation, it is actually better if a person grabs you - you can manipulate their structure much easier from this position and use them against their partner.

What if your partners are throwing punches, can we still join them? Yes, we can! With the same set up, A and B feed in slow punches and kicks. C moves as before, trying not to get caught in between the two. C also now works to deflect any attacks, but also pushes them towards the other partner. To illustrate, we have A throw the hook punch. C ducks under it a little, deflecting with the arm. C now helps the punch on its way, towards B's face. This can be surprisingly effective if you get your timing right. It might even start a new fight between A and B!

If you want to expand this out a little, just have a group of everyone punching everyone else. This is very good preparation

for crowd work, footwork, taking and giving hits and redirecting attacks. It's one of the drills we use a lot, when a larger group is available, To outsides it may seem scrappy, but I've found nothing that prepares you better for a real-life "punch-up" than this. Of course, levels of intensity can be varied, as we will detail in a later chapter.

For now, let's return to our two attackers and look at some timing issues. People rarely work in complete synch. For all sorts of reasons, if you have two attackers one will always move before the other. We can take advantage of this to work against the slower person. The drill starts as before, A and B fronting up C. Let's say A launches the first attack. C immediately moves to B and strikes, takes down, makes a shield, or whatever work is to be applied. This has the effect of not only neutralising A's attack, it also usually catches B by surprise.

Of course, we also think back to our earlier timing drills and simply add in an extra person or two. Your response doesn't have to be attack, it may be that the better option is to create distance, especially if we are outnumbered. But how to do this effectively? Let's imagine we are confronted by two young attackers out in the open. We could turn and run, but to do so we have to turn our back, and, more to the point, are we fast and fit enough to outrun them?

Again, much is dependant on circumstances, but I would suggest that if you have people close enough to attack you, the time to turn and escape has already gone. If we want to create distance from that position, it is best to do something against the attackers first, as detailed above, at least that may give you some extra time.

If we want to escape, there are a number of factors to consider. What is the environment - urban, rural, indoors? In a city setting it is usually easier to escape. There are shops to dodge into, crowds to hide in, lots of street furniture and cars to hide behind and so on. Back in the day in London it was easy to jump on a bus, they had an open door at the back. Mind you, I also once saw a great fight at a bus stop started by guys jumping off the bus and into the queue, but that's another story! On the downside, it is not so easy to run in that setting, lots of obstacles, traffic, etc.

In a rural setting there may be more space to run, but less places to hide! However, if you know how to use the landscape it can be surprisingly easy to disappear, especially in low light.

As we mentioned last chapter, consider how many people there are around. Will they help? Can you go into a shop and ask them to call the police? Nowadays, at the very least, someone will likely film any incident on their phone, even if they don't come to your direct aid.

How well do you know your surroundings? If you are on home turf you should have a good knowledge of the best places to run, hide, etc. Or you may be in a new environment, in which case think back to our awareness work. You should have already scanned the area for likely escape routes, etc.

Consider the motivation of your attackers, too. What are the stakes involved, are they looking for an easy robbery target, or is this a personal issue. I'm reminded of the story of the fox chasing the rabbit - the fox is running for its dinner, the rabbit for its life. This is another reason why it pays to remain emotionally in control - you don't want to give people any extra reason to

attack you. I've seen situations that were going off the boil flare up again because one "mouth" starts throwing insults again.

Who is with you? If you are on your own and reasonably fit, running might be a good option. If you have kids, partner, parents, etc with you, then perhaps not. If your child is very young, can you pick them up and run? It's an interesting exercise to run while carrying something bulky, not only as possible preparation but as a general way of learning to work efficiently

People make much of running if confronted by a knife. Now, I'm not going into knife defence in his book, but I will just add this. Try this experiment. Give your partner a training knife and place them around ten feet away. Tell them that as soon as you turn and start to run, they can begin stabbing. You will find that in the time it takes you to turn, they will already be on you, and, what's more, you

ourselves in a crowd - sporting or music events, rush hour travel, a busy street, demonstrations and marches, and so on. Situations here can become extremely dangerous, as the crowd takes on a life of its own. This is often not even caused by violence but by other factors - fire, panic, etc - resulting in loss of life in some cases.

The first thing we need to be aware of, is the mood of the crowd. Be receptive to what is going on around you, keep your eyes up and scanning. I've found that you can quite easily read a crowd and judge its mood. Listen - are people laughing, singing joking, or shouting in anger or fear? These are quite obvious indicators but there are more subtle ones too.

now have your back to them. So again, without doing something first, or evading from a greater distance, the odds aren't good.

Overall, then, if you need to escape, think ahead as you go, try and work out the best route or places to hide and, most importantly, work your mobility. This is where training outdoors comes into its own, in all sorts of environments. Pre lockdown we were planning an urban workshop, just to give people a taste of moving through a different environment. Failing that, just go for a run in a place where there are some obstacles to go over, round, under or through. It's a good exercise for general fitness in any case.

CROWD WORK

There are numerous times where we find

In my younger days I was present at some demonstrations in London. It was educational to see how crowds could be directed and led, whether by the organisers or by provocateurs. It's also interesting to see that how a crowd is treated can make a big difference. Pen people in and frighten them and you will often turn them aggressive. The best events are well managed, with routes and boundaries clearly marked and people treated with respect.

I was once at a large music venue, watching a well known rock group. A steward was literally shouting and screaming at people, telling them to "sit down and stop dancing." At a rock concert, where people have paid a lot of money to have a good time! Eventually, a rather large chap advised the steward of some possible outcomes to his interference and the hi-viz jacket man retreated, perhaps to consider his future career options.

The next factor to consider in a crowd is movement. Now, the major difficulty in practicing any crowd work is in finding a crowd! To some extent you can go out and work in a real crowd, failing that, you can simulate to some extent with fewer people but in a confined space. However, particularly at workshops, we may get the opportunity to work with upwards of a hundred people.

The first drill is simply to move through the crowd as softly as possible, Try to avoid contact or, where you do get contact, slip around it. Imagine you are water, you offer minimal resistance, you flow through the gaps.

From there, you can make things more active. Have people in the crowd grappling or fighting each other in some way. It is the job of others to go round them without getting dragged into the fight. You can give people tasks. For example, in a crowd of thirty, give five of them the task of

working through the crowd to reach a certain spot, escape out through a door, and so on. The crowd don't actively stop them, as such, but they can make things awkward for the people coming through.

Practice moving through the crowd while carrying something - a medicine ball, plastic cups filled with water and so on. This will help with your movement and sensitivity.

Should you find yourself struggling to move through a crowd, then try some of these drills with a smaller group. Let's say one person against six. First, have the six stand around you and jostle you a bit. Get used to going with the flow, though without losing your structure.

Next, have the six stand a row facing you, quite close together. You have to move through them, weaving in and out. Increase

the speed as your movement becomes smoother. You can add in grabs or strikes as you see fit.

Next, have the six stand in a line, facing you. They should be shoulder to shoulder. Your job is to go through the line - not by barging, but by slipping through the gaps. So take a moment and look to see where the gaps are. You may be able to scoot between someone's legs, or you may be able to step through a gap between hips. Your aim is to disturb the group as little as possible.

Being on the floor in a crowd is an unpleasant experience! Revisit our earlier floor drill, have part of your group on the ground while the rest "fight" above. The standing people are not actively working against those on the floor, nor should they be too careful about stepping on them. Those on the floor move as best they can to protect themselves. At a signal, those on the floor stand as quickly as they can, take the nearest person down to the floor and continue the drill.

Should you be caught in a panicking crowd, awareness of your surroundings is once again key. Are there places that you can slip into that will protect you from a crush? Can you climb up onto something, for example? You should already have some idea of escape routes, can you work through the crowd to one of those?

If we have to be active in a crowd, there are two approaches to take. Once is to create space, the other is to work against those closest to you. For the first, we can go into wide, swinging movements, using a figure eight pattern or similar. If you do this with enough enthusiasm, you will likely create some space around you. The downsides are that you can damage your hand if it hits a hard skull and you also draw a lot of attention to yourself.

We drill this by having a person in the middle of the group with some big boxing gloves on. At the signal, they "go", and it is up to the people around them to avoid the strikes! It is important that this kind of work is unrestrained, to some extent the wilder the swings the more people tend to back off!

The other approach uses short work in order to strike, takedown or control someone right next to you. This is more subtle and should go largely unnoticed by those around. The person can then be used as a shield, removed from the crowd, neutralised or whatever is called for in the situation.

SEATED WORK

Consider where most martial arts training takes place - a nice hall, well lit, with mats and heating. Then consider where 99% of incidents take place - in a crowded bar, on a train, in your car. So let's see how we can work in some of those situations. We will start by looking at working from a seated position. Now, there are a number of ways we can use the chair itself, which we will cover in the section on improvised weapons. Before that, we will start with working from the chair.

There are obvious pros and cons to working from a seated position. We don't have to worry about balance, but we are not that mobile. This gives us some clues as to how to work. One very good way is to use our legs against our attackers legs. We remain stable, they lose their balance. Think back to our ground work against the legs. A sits in the chair, B stands in front.

A uses their hands and/or feet to work against B's knees, ankles and hips. The idea is to get a feel for how the joints work, how a leg can be locked in order to make the person stumble or fall. Once you have worked static, next have B walk in. Start to carefully apply the work.

From there, have B become more active - they can come in and grab or strike A, for example. A again works the legs. Once A starts taking B's balance, they can work

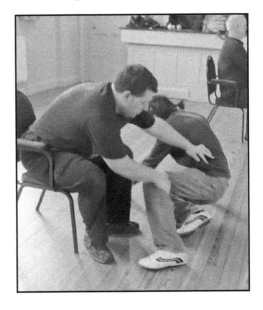

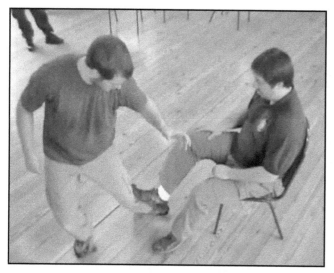

or have it ready to pick up as a shield. Next, consider how you stand up and sit down. Ideally, you would do this in one movement. Look at how most people get up from a chair - they lean forward, put hands on knees and push up from there. Put this into a self defence context - you are offering any attacker your chain and keeping your hands down!

Instead, imagine you are being pulled up by the crowd of the head. You keep the spine straight and lift from the seat, with hands ready. The same goes for sitting down. Reference the chair with the backs of your legs, then sit as though you were doing a squat.

against the upper body. See how, for example, if A kicks the knee, B bends forward. A can now grab an arm and apply a hold or takedown.

This is largely static work but we also need to know how to move on, off and around the chair. Start by simply walking around the chair while keeping in contact with it. You may want to use the chair as a barrier,

After that, consider other ways of getting off the chair. Allow your hips to slide out, relax the body and slip off the chair. This is a good way of getting from chair to floor quickly and safely. It also has other applications. Say a

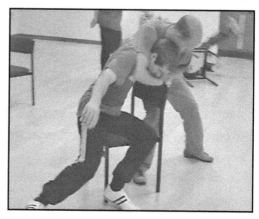

person has grabbed you from behind, or tries to put a choke on you. One way to escape is to drop a shoulder and slide down. If you grab the attacking arm you may even be able to drag the attacker with you. Let the weight of the body free you from the hold, no need to apply tension.

Other ways of moving help us to use the chair directly against a person. In the above situation, if you sense the person approaching from behind, stand and sharply push the chair back into them with your legs.

There's also two methods for standing and using the chair. For the first, have your feet outside the front legs of the chair and grab the front of the seat. As you stand, pull the chair up and forward, to throw at a person, or use as a shield.

For the second, wrap one foot around the leg of the chair. As you stand, kick out with that foot, so spinning the chair out. Lift the back of the chair at the same time and

again, the chair becomes a shield or missile. Sometimes we may have to move back quickly, to evade an attack or if we cannot go forward. To practice this, sit in the chair, then lean back until the front legs are off the

floor. Bend the body forward slightly, then let the chair fall back. As the back of the chair contacts the ground, go into a backward roll. This is a good fear exercise, too, letting yourself go back at that balance point. It's best to have some experience of rolling on the ground before trying this. Also, remember to practice jumping over chairs, o r

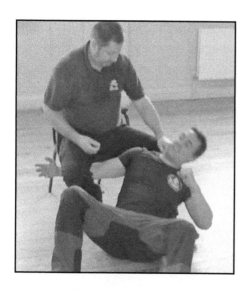

similar obstacles, whether it is a jump on and off, or whether it's a full dive over.

This is good training to do in all of our environment, indoor and outdoor. As we have mentioned, people talk about running away as an option, but are you able to navigate any obstacles as you do so. Practicing dives and rolls over chairs and the like will increase your confidence and ability.

Of course, we can practice all our usual punching, locking and takedown work from the chair too. If you have trained in Systema punching methods, which don't rely on a stance, you should be able to deliver powerful strikes from seated as well as standing positions. You can train at first simply by having partners feed in attacks while you have to remain in the chair. See again how the chair, while it compromises

mobility, gives you a very stable base from which to work.

CAR WORK

One time where we are sitting down is while driving! Add to this the incidents of road rage that we can all get involved in from time to time, and it makes sense to study how to work in and around your vehicle.

The start point, as always, is mobility. Look at how you enter and exit your vehicle. As with standing from the chair, do you offer your chin and tie up your hands when getting out? One way to exit safely is to swing your legs out, then use your nearest elbow against the door jamb to lever yourself out of the driving seat. This brings you out in one move and allows you to keep your hands up.

Next, sit in your driver's seat and see what mobility you have. Twist, turn, get used to being mobile in your own car. After that, see if you can move to the passenger seat smoothly, then from front to back. Can you enter or exit your car through the windows?

Again, self defence does not cover just physical assault but also traffic accidents and other situations. As I write, we had a speeding car overturn outside the house just a couple of days ago. The lady was trapped inside (fortunately not injured and she was extricated safely). Imagine if no-one had been around, though. In this situation it pays to know how to get quickly out of your car in unconventional ways!

next set of traffic lights, they jump out to let you know their feelings. We should first consider the other person - is this a serious attack, or just someone venting verbals steam? If the latter, don't get involved. Keep the window up, the car locked.

As you move, be aware of all the fixtures and fittings, too. Sleeves can get snagged on handbrakes. Seatbelts can entangle, or be used to entangle another person. How do all the seat controls work? In short, you should know the interior of your vehicle as well as the interior of your house - after all, you are just as, or even more likely, to be in a situation while in it than many other places.

Incidents around a car work in one of three ways. One person is in the car, one outside. Or, both may be outside the car, perhaps a robbery situation, or if you have left the car to confront someone. The third is where both people are in the car - it could be a rowdy passenger, a carjacker or similar. As we have just been studying seated work, let's start with the first.

So, you are in your car, you upset another driver and, at the

If they move to close range, be prepared. If you have the window wound up, they may not be able to attack you, but might take it out on the car. Can you escape safely? Or you could film them on your phone, being sure to get their licence plate in the shot, too.

If your window is down, there are many things we can do should they decide to assault us. The advantage we have is that an attacker has to reach in to grab or punch. Let them. Grab the wrist and see how you can use the door/ window edge as a lever

same work applies, but also think now how you can use the door itself. Trapping a person's hand against the sill and opening the door wider gives you a lot of leverage. Doors can be shut on hands / fingers, or you can use the door to bang into a person's leg.

against the elbow. If you push the incoming hand towards the windscreen, you will likely bring the attacker's head close to the door, bringing it in range of your other hand.

Should an attacker reach in with both hands to grab, again, let them. They now have both hands tied up, you can reach out to strike / control their head. A sharp pull will bring the forehead in contact with the car door.

A steering wheel can be used to lock a person's wrist and arm. You may direct the hand there from a grab, or people may even directly reach in to grab it. Either way, pull the hand into the gap between the spokes, then turn the wheel a little to lock the wrist. This may be useful if you have to detain someone while calling the police, for example.

What if your car door is open? Perhaps the attacker opens it, or catches you on the way in or out. The

Of course, we can turn this situation around - what if you need to get a person out of a car? This is more usually a situation a professional may face, but we will give a couple of ideas here.

Assuming we have the door open, the simplest way is to grab the person's arm, bring the elbow to the door jamb and exert pressure. This will almost always "pop" the person out of the seat. If the person is gripping the steering wheel, don't try and pull the hands free. Instead, slide onto their

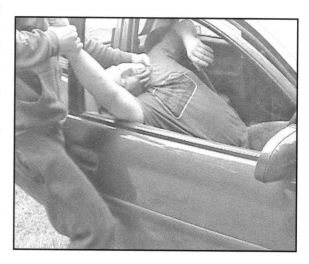

fingertips and pull one or two fingers back individually.

Head control is another good method - I've seen someone extracted out through an open car window by their ears!

One last method for now, again if the door is open. Place your foot behind the person's outer ankle, and lift it out of the car. If you flick the leg up, it should come outside the car and hang there. Then close the door on their shin. It's not a nice thing to do, but in a pinch it will disable a person long enough for you to carry out other work.

What if we are attacked outside our car? Again, much depends on the context. It may be a robbery attempt, or perhaps someone with a grudge who followed you out of the bar. We refer back to our awareness training, as well as thinking of things like having our keys ready and car unlocked, so we can be in and away as quickly as possible. Another situation may be a road rage incident, where we get out to confront someone, or for other reasons. In all cases, we can use the car. It;s most obvious use is as a big shield to place between us and an attacker.

A car also has numerous sharp edges, particularly if a door is open. Pushing an attacker's head into one of these will have an effect- though only in the most serious of situations, and take great care when practicing.

Whether to stay or get out of your car is a difficult question to answer. Generally, I would advise against it. If you've upset another motorist, is it worth getting into

137

a scrap over something so trivial? Most people will shout and bluster then, ego satisfied, leave you alone. On the other hand, if the person truly wishes you harm, or takes your kindness as weakness, it may be that we have to exit and deal with them.

If you do, be aware of how you exit the car. You don't want to be halfway out and have the person slam your own door on you. On the other hand, you may be able to hit them with the door to push them back. The time to get out is as they are approaching, usually. Once they are at your door you may be better off controlling them from your seated position. Of course, another simple fact is that a person outside a car is very vulnerable to a moving car. But I wouldn't for one second condone driving at them.

Another possible scenario is having someone in the car with you. The first thing to do to prevent this, is to always check the back seat of your car before you get in. It's not a common scenario in my experience, but, in any event, we should always be sure to lock our car, even if away from it for just a moment. If you do see someone in the back, create distance and call the police.

Should you have to deal with someone in the car, they will be in one of two positions - next to you or behind you. A more common situation in the UK was for someone to slip into the passenger seat at traffic lights to rob the driver or steal the car. So keep your car doors locked when out travelling, particularly in town. Also, if it's hot and you have the windows down, be aware of having valuables on display and within reach. A bag on a seat is easily snatched through an open window while you are stationary.

If a person gets in your car, what are they after? Are they armed? What is their mental state? If you need to work against them, then obviously, the work needs to be short and sharp. So practice striking, applying locks, etc in that position. Have your partner in the passenger seat and behind, applying strikes, grabbing you, threatening with the knife and so on. Think back to our earlier work with the steering wheel. Again, it is quite straightforward to use it to lock an arm.

Also explore working with the seatbelt. It

can be used to tie up or even choke a person with a little practice. Finally, look at how you can jam a person into awkward positions in the footwell, or how you can disrupt their movement by quickly adjusting seats (yours or theirs). If someone has grabbed you from the rear seat, sharply push the driver seat back into them to gain some time.

This supposes that the car is stationary. If you are driving, obviously that takes precedence over any other action. But check if the passenger has their belt on - will a sudden stop throw them into the dashboard? In more extreme cases, you might do all you can to attract attention, even to the extent of crashing into another vehicle.

In common with all our work, the key to gaining abilities in these situations is through running simple drills. Start with movement, then add in a partner or two. Being with working against simple, slow attacks and explore all the possibilities available to you. People sometimes look only at the limitations of being in a car, or similar. Instead, we learn to look at the options that any environment gives us. Plus, of course, we never neglect the options of avoidance, de-escalation, or talking our way out. Those should always be our first priority.

CONFINED SPACE

When you think about it, most situations are likely to involve some kind of obstacle or impediment to our movement. Even outside in the street, there will be a wall, a kerbstone, a lamppost.

Once again, the simplest way to prepare for this is to train in those environments. Even if your regular training is in a large, spacious hall, I'm betting there is a doorway, a lobby, maybe a toilet. Our local halls have a small kitchen, sometimes stairs, usually a car park. We have run workshops in a local bar/club around the tables and chairs. These are all areas to train in and, as with the car, become aware of the increased possibilities such spaces give us.

If you train in a hall, is there any furniture you can place around? Put chairs and tables out and have the group move around, under, and over them. Then begin your normal drills

- be they one on one or group - in amongst the furniture. You can set it up randomly, or you could simulate being in a cinema or similar.

Of course, take particular care when working on stairs. Here, we will most often be other above or below our attacker. If the latter, see how you can easily grab a foot and pull the person down. If above be aware of the foot grab and see how much closer your attacker's head is to your foot!

give you support and, if you are pushed, you can minimise danger from the fall by sliding down the wall.

Moving up and down stairs safely is an important skill, not only for confrontation but if you are caught in a fire. At the top of the stair, get on your front and slowly slide down. This way, you stay low to the ground and can move quickly without fear of falling. In terms of defence, explore - carefully - how you can push or throw a person down the stairs. One tip here is to keep one side of your body in contact with the wall. It will

WALL TRAINING

How about if we have a wall to our front or back. For the first, here is a pushing drill that is very useful. A stands in front of the wall, B pushes them into it. Start quite close and with not too much force.

A treats the wall as the floor - think back to how we fell forward. The arms extend then, as one contacts the wall, you fold and

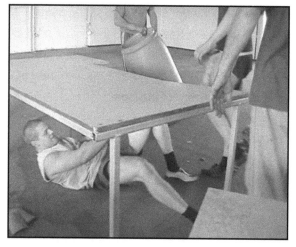

rotate it, taking your body out to the side. Your back should contact the wall, you can then push off of it back to the pusher. The harder they push, the quicker you come back.

After that, A has their back to the wall and B again pushes. This time, on impact A should round their shoulders out, using that movement to "bounce" off of the wall. Try it softly at first, once you get the feel you will be able to take a hard push with no problem. Almost imagine you are hitting the wall with your back rather than it hitting you. Naturally, exhaling also helps!

A common situation is to be pinned against the wall. We have already discussed some possibilities, but I wanted to go over this again in order to illustrate how we apply principles in a practical way.

So let's set up a simple scenario, A has B pushed up against the wall. Step one, is for B to be in control of their mental state, through breathing.

Step two B should recognise both the pros

and cons of being in this position. For example:

Pros - has support from the wall, can only go forward, can use the wall as a weapon.

Cons - limited room to strike, fear and tension from attacker's aggression, can only go forward.

Step three is to understand context. Is this a domination move by a bully? A robbery? A pretext to sexual assault? And so on. Obviously, our response needs to be appropriate. From this position it is easy to reach up to the eyes, for example. But is it right to blind someone who's just being a bit stroppy? On the other hand, if your life is at stake, a shove may not be enough to deter your attacker.

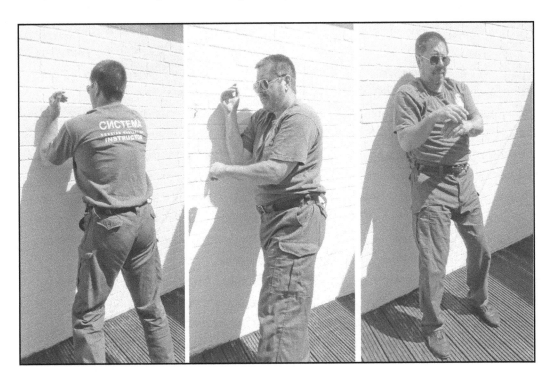

Once we have an idea of our level of response, we can begin to implement it. What do you want to achieve? If it is simply to escape, then we look at our work against locks and holds. From that, we know that one part of a grip or hold will always be weakest. This is the point we escape towards. In the case of being pinned, the arms are strong in the pushing direction -

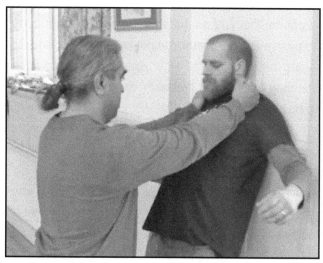

so pushing back is a waste of time. However, if we duck under an arm and step, we are moving against the weak point of the attacker's structure. We are also moving into a space. This is another important concept for any type of evasion or escape. Look for the gap, or where the space will be, and move into it.

Another option is to work against the attacker's structure, relatively softly. We have already looked at working the legs. From this position we might grab under the attacker's arms and, using a figure eight or wave from the shoulders, move them aside. We may place one hand to the hip, then come over with the other to manipulate the head, so bending the spine.

We may even simply quickly drop, using our bodyweight to bend the attacker forward. Whatever we do, we must be ready to take advantage of the unbalancing of the opponent, either following up with a

strike, a push or a break free and escape.

There is also the option of striking. A person with both hands on your chest is vulnerable to a strike to the ribs, or solar plex. You may try hitting the head, but raising the hands up will likely trigger a blocking response in the other person. Of course, we don't have to stop at one strike. Even if the first only disrupts our attacker, it brings us time to throw in more strikes.

A final physical option is to use pain compliance to make the attacker move. If wearing short sleeves, reach up and grab a small piece of skin under each arm. Twist sharply. Or perhaps poke two fingers into the throat - in and down should make most people move back.

Another effective option is to grab skin at the person's sides - the muffin tops! Twist one hand forward and one hand back, it is surprisingly painful.

Hit with the edge of the hand sharply under the nose Again, we take advantage of the time and space gained to follow up or attack.

This all pre-supposes we have tried our first option, which is always to talk our way out. However, knowing you have all these other options to fall back on, will increase the confidence you have in any "negotiation." And generally, if we are this stage, the time for talking has already passed, though you can use your actions to back up your words and vice-versa.

This is an easy situation to drill. Simply have your partner grab your jacket and pin you against the wall. Work slowly through all the various physical options, see what you find most effective. Be aware that, especially with pain compliance, levels of tolerance can differ widely. Also take into account clothing - pinching will do nothing through a thick coat, for example.

Now, at first this might all seem a bit clinical, a bit analytical, a little slow. That's okay, we are learning. Over time, these choices and options will become apparent very quickly - as long as you maintain that even mindset. Panic usually leads to ineffective thrashing about and makes the situation

worse. Keep calm, be assertive in your actions and always be ready to adapt.

Techniques are not magic keys which work regardless, so we are always ready to change, to switch. If a movement doesn't work the first time, it won't work the second. Repeating it over and over won't help. If you are working high, switch low. If you are trying to control the head and there is a lot of resistance, drive a knee into the thigh, then go back to the head again. Understand not only your own tensions, but those of your attacker.

This is the blueprint for much of our self defence work and we will examine how to set up and adjust these drills in a later chapter. You can apply them to being on the floor, in a phone box, anything and everything, as the principles are universal.

When working in a normal rather than "nice

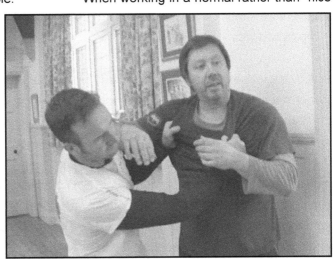

mats" environment, also consider what is around. Are there objects you can push people into or over? Can you close a door on fingers? Is the person stood at the top of a slope, will a shove back send them flying? Again, with awareness and observation you will come to recognise the tactical advantages of any environment and learn to use them to your advantage.

IMPROVISED WEAPONS

When talk turns to self defence, there are three very common phrases that crop up which always have me rolling my eyes. They are:

1. I'd just run
2. I'd just kick him in the balls
3. I'd have my keys ready in my hand.

We have already spoken about running and kicking with power and precision takes considerable practice. It's the third statement we will look at now, in the context of improvised weapons.

First, by improvised weapons we mean any general, everyday item that comes to hand. In a sense, this is another aspect of using our environment. Most usually, people think of a walking stick, a belt, or those ever-popular keys. There are a number of commercially available items, often prefixed with the word *tactical* that are sold specifically as improvised weapons, things

like pens, key rings, kubotans and so on. For the most part I have little time for such items. They are often expensive, perform in the same way as most household items and, despite the cool *tactical* tag, are not a magic item that instantly levels the playing field against an aggressive attacker.

This is a very important point to bear in mind. Carrying a weapon of any kind can give a psychological boost and an increase in confidence. That is all well and good but the confidence does not necessarily spill over into ability. The item itself does not bestow any skills or powers. From any perspective, it is the person that is dangerous, not the weapon.

Keys in the fist is a prime example. I've had people with absolutely no confrontation experience tell me this - "I'll be okay, I'll have my keys in my fist." Depending on the situation, I usually ask "Have you ever punched anyone?" If not, why would having keys in your fist make any difference?

Even if you land a hit, will you hurt your wrist? Will you hurt your assailant enough to stop them, or just annoy them? Worse still, what happens when you hurt your hand, flinch and drop your keys? You've just handed your attacker your house and car keys.

If you want to use keys - if you want to use anything - you have to have a base to work from. The beauty of Systema is that our principle-led approach means all our usual movements work just as well with an item. We don't need to learn a book kata, or a belt form. So our approach to improvised weapons is this - *do I have good movement, can I work effectively from close range*, and so on. Then, it may be I have a pen in my hand, so *what can I do with it?*

This also lessens the psychological attachment to any weapon - should we drop or lose it, it's not a big deal, we don't feel lost without it. Given that, what I will do here is run through some potential items and give some pointers on how to use them.

Much as with our environment, we want to highlight the pros while being aware of the cons. To some extent, this work is partly covered in *Systema Locks, Throws and Holds*, but I will repeat some of the ideas there in case you don't have that book. We can broadly divide improvised weapons into three categories, Flexible, Solid and Missile.

FLEXIBLE

A belt is the most common item here. Easy to carry, it can be slipped off in a second. It gives good reach, potentially has a heavy buckle for damage at one end, and can wrap up, even restrain, an attacker. On the other hand, a belt can be grabbed and used against you, it may not cause enough harm to stop someone and you might have to hold your pants up with one hand while you fight!

First things first, with any item. Get used to deploying and handling it. How fast can you get the belt off? Can you swing it around without hitting yourself in the face? Get used to striking with it - hang a target off a clothes line, or use a dummy or similar, and see how accurate you can be with the buckle.

A word on how to hold the belt for striking. Don't wrap it round your fist, if someone grabs the other end they have control of your arm. Instead drape the belt over your palm as shown. Now rotate your palm to thumb down. From there, rotate up again, looping the belt over your palm. This gives you a

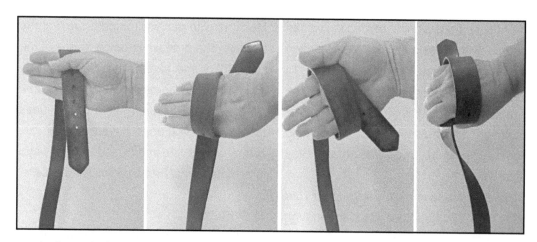

good grip on the belt, but if someone grabs it, you only have to straighten your fingers to slip out.

In this mode, the belt can be used to keep an attacker at bay, or clear some space in a crowd. Just be aware that, unless you have a hefty buckle, you are unlikely to do significant damage to anyone, so the belt is more for controlling distance than anything else.

Another way to strike with the belt is to fold it in half and hold both ends. We then use the flat of the belt to hit with a sharp pull of the wrists. This can create space if a person has grabbed you, hit to the forehead, across the eyes, or into the throat. In a similar way, strike into the crook of a grabbing arm, the weakest point of the structure, to push the arm away. This will work against a grab or, with good timing, a strike. Again, this method won't cause damage but should create a physical and

psychological gap that you can take advantage of.

The third use of the belt is in wrapping movements to either help break structure or to tie up an opponent. Obvious places to loop the belt are round the neck, the wrist, the crook of the elbow, behind the knee. Any of this positions will give you a good handle to work with. With practice, you will be able to wrap an attacking hand, then loop an end

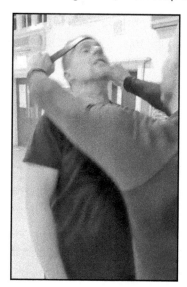

round the neck, effectively wrapping the person up. Pulling sharply down and out of the base of support will then bring the person to the floor.

It can be tempting, with wrapping work, to try and make elaborate loops, to keep going on and on, almost as though you were a spider wrapping something in a web. Be sure to keep things simple and straightforward. Remember, you have to work these skills under pressure and, unless you have huge amounts of time to devote to practicing one particular thing, it is better to be a jack of all trades when it comes to using improvised weapons. Again, these are simple things we pick up to help us in a tricky situation, nothing more.

There are other similar items we can use in the same way - a length of chord or rope, perhaps even the wire on a set of headphones. A heavier flexible item, such

as a chain, is more sorted to swinging and hitting work, which is easily practiced. They also make good exercise items, as detailed in our other books. I suppose a whip also falls under the category of flexible weapon, and a very effective one too (as well as being useful for massage!) However the whip really is a weapon rather than an improvised weapon so we shall not cover that here. Instead, let's move on to solid items.

SOLID WEAPONS

Under this category we can places things like a stick, a book, pens, keys, and so on. Their primary use is in various types of striking work, but can also be useful in reinforcing locks. The use of them in restraint work is covered elsewhere, so we shall

mostly look at other applications here - besides which, in a self defence situation our priority is generally to break free and escape.

The stick, or maybe the rock, is the oldest known weapon. Usually to hand, easy to use, effective. Hitting someone over the head with a big stick will obviously get a result, though in our self defence context, we must again be aware of legalities. This was reinforced by two cases here in the UK. In the most recent, a man was attacked by three others, intent on doing him serious harm. They were armed with clubs and a knife. The lone man managed to get the knife off of one attacker and stabbed all three. He was cleared of all charges in court as he had effectively been fighting for his life. Incidentally, the incident that spurred this vicious attack was an argument at a family wedding!

The other case, a year or two back, was that of a shop owner chasing a robber from his store. He caught up with the man at the end of the street and set about him with a cricket bat. The shop keeper was charged for that - he was in no danger at the time he attacked and his target was running away. So, while a cricket or baseball bat is an effective and handy weapon, be aware of how and when you might use one.

There are whole martial arts devoted to

stick work, but we are keeping with our theme of jack-of-all-trades. So simply pick up a stick or bat and start working with it. Get the feel and balance firs, then start working figure eight patterns. The stick is a great exercises tool in any case, for mobility and strength training. Keep your movements big to start with, stretch yourself out. Then bring the movements in to a more practical range. It's also good to move with the stick in more confined spaces - within a doorway, for example. If in the house, remove any breakables beforehand!

Don't forget to move around as you use the stick, don't be glued on the spot. In many ways striking with the stick follows all the same principles of striking with the hand. You can use long wave movement, or short, sharp hits - think of the stick as a drumstick hitting a drum (not the chicken kind!) Rap with a sharp twist of the wrist, see how much power you can develop. You can work against a pad, a post, or a stick held by another partner.

Also be sure to work with different types of stick, or whatever you might choose to carry in your car. In other words, familiarise yourself with whatever you are most likely to have to hand in a situation. If in the car, it is best to have a use for the stick. Perhaps you like to play baseball at the local park? Maybe, like me, you are knocking on a bit and need a walking stick...

For targets, we usually look at bony areas - the back of the hand, knees, shins, collarbone and head (with the caveat that strikes to the head can cause serious damage.) But also think about working the muscles. A heavier item, such as a truncheon, works well into the upper arm or upper leg muscles. Of course we can also use the end of the stick to prod into areas such as the throat.

The next stage is to start working (softly) on a partner. Have them static at first, then gradually add in movement. You can work to keep distance - against a knife attack, you might stay back and hit the hand, for example. Remember, the stick is not a magic bullet, you still need to work your movement, positioning and angles.

Also, as with our empty hand striking, work to develop short hits with the stick, try not to rely on big swings. The other option is to hit with the end of the stick using a hammer fist type attack. This will also work, to some extent, with objects such as pens, etc.

Next, try using the stick against grabs. You can start with strikes, using the end again, or holding each end of the stick and striking

into the face. Another simple movement is to flick the stick into the groin to help break the grip and escape.

As we mentioned, the stick can also reinforce movement. Have your partner grab you, or hold a knife against your body. Place the stick against the wrist and roll down, pulling back slightly. It should release the grip and pin the hand against your body.

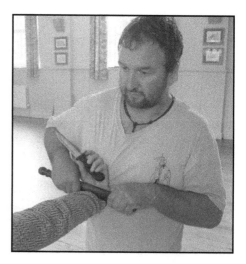

If your partner grabs with both hands, either work into the inside crease of the elbow, or work the "over/under" principle. This is something to try whenever you work against two arms - they might be holding something, they might be holding you! Go over one arm

and under the other, this gives you good leverage in order to take the person's balance. Remember, apply movement from your shoulders and with a short step, don't try and muscle through with tension.

While we are on the subject of sticks, let's look at some ways of working against them, too. After all, a stick or a bat is a very common weapon, easy to carry and use. We will start with a flow drill.

Partner A pushes partner B with the stick. B relaxes to absorb the push, using that movement to bring the hands up into position. From here, B takes the stick from A, then, quickly as possible, pushes A back. It is now A's turn to absorb, disarm and return the attack.

At first, don't apply too much resistance, the initial aim is to get the feel of how to take the stick. There are three ways to do this. First, we work against the stick. Grab close to each end, feel how much leverage this gives you against your partner's grip. Turn from your shoulders, and at the same time twist the stick.

The second method is to work against the hands. Move in and slide your hands to contact your partner's. You can either work against the fingers, push into the inside of the wrist, or even trap the hand in place and lock it with the stick.

The third method is to ignore the stick, evade it altogether, and work directly against the

positions to be in - outside of the curve (safe but can't reach the attacker), directly on the curve (where we take the blow full force), inside the curve (less impact and we can reach the attacker.)

So have a partner feed in swings and hits and, first off, try to maintain distance, work outside the curve. Be constantly moving, keep your hands in close, protect your head. Next, work on moving to inside the circle. As the bat comes up, move into the person. You may be able to jam their arms, or go for head control, strike, etc.

person. You might go for head control, or work to the legs, even grab the jacket. As you get used to the drill you can add in more resistance, and also work in things like level changes, strikes and so on.

From there, progress to working against stick strikes. The most important thing here is our timing. Let's look at a typical "bat swing". The person pulls back to strike, then hits out in a curve. There are three

If you need to, use the arms in a kind of "roof shape" to protect the head. Think of a wedge, anything that hits it will hopefully slide off - if we are moving! On no account try to block an overhead strike with your arm, it will get damaged.

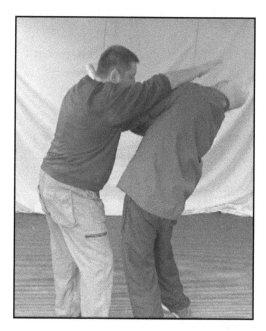

blow there can have devastating results. Once you have your movement and timing, begin working against your partner. You may strike, duck and attack the legs, work into takedowns and so on. If you think back to our first drill, you will also find that taking the stick is an option, too.

A word on using the stick, how we carry it, how we deploy it. The typical method for a stick or baton is one hand out, the stick raised ready. It is meant to intimidate, I suppose. Personally, I find this limits my options. I am showing the person where my strike is going. I've also found that sticking a hand in someone's face rarely calms then down!

For your timing, think back to our earlier pre-emptive and movement work. Watch your partner's body language and predict the angle where possible. Rather than try and avoid the stick, work into the spaces where it isn't.

It is possible to absorb some of the power of a hit if absolutely necessary. We may get caught out, or may be unable to move or dodge. Think back to the earlier work on taking kicks and strikes. If you can, use the arm as a barrier and, as the stick hits, rotate it in the same direction as the force. The arm may get injured, but better that than the head or ribs.

I can' t stress enough, against any stick or bat attack, you must protect the head, preferably by movement. Even a "soft"

So an alternative is to hide the stick. It might be concealed down the leg, or behind the arm. In low light, it can be concealed against the body in order to hide its outline. In all cases, the stick is easily deployed and used. You will also notice the other hand is ready, but not overtly so.

Experiment with these positions, see how you can quickly strike from each, often from a less predictable angle. I always find that learning how to deploy and use a weapon considerably improves our awareness of how other people carry and use them too - so bear that in mind if a person ever stands like this in front of you!

Items such as books and keys can also be used to hit. Obviously we are using the sharp corners or edges of these items to get a reaction. Work into the appropriate target areas again - soft areas, the ribs, the back of the head.

Pressure points are a topic that often comes up in self defence, but they come with a caveat. Not everyone reacts to pressure point attacks. A typical example might be against a grab. You can dig a key sharply into the point just inside the forearm at the elbow. You might get a good reaction with one person, another will shrug it off.

By all means, study pressure points, but your primary targets should be the obvious weak areas - eyes, throat, etc. It is also possible

to reinforce this type of strike by pushing into the target from the opposite direction - though, of course, this will prevent the person from moving back. Again, our main goal here is to buy to time to break free and escape.

Our procedure is the same. First get used to deploying the item and handling it. If you are going to use keys, then please don't use your house/car keys - buy a set of hefty old keys from a junk store and use those. Next, work your target areas on a partner. Apply pressure and see what works best. See how we can use an attack in one place to set up a flow of continuous movement. So you might rap the back of the hand sharply to make that hand withdraw, then follow up with a strike to the face. Again, the weapon is not necessarily the thing that will finish the job, but it may help you get there.

While we are on the subject of books, I'll also mention magazines. These were used in two ways "back in the day." The first was to use something like a thick catalogue or similar as a crude form of body armour. If a person thought there might be knives involved, they would sometimes tuck such an item into their waistband - for those of a certain age, it was usually an Argos catalogue! Crude, but it did give some measure of protection against a stab to the guts.

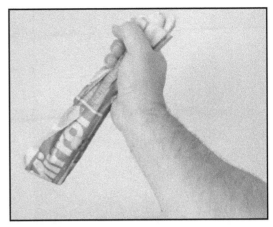

The second item is the near-mythical Millwall Brick. This came about during the height of football hooliganism in the UK. Spectators were searched on going into a ground and items like sharpened combs, etc confiscated. If you were wearing steel toecap boots, the police would make you remove the laces. To get round this, some bright spark took in a harmless newspaper, rolled it up tight, then folded it in half. This formed a hard object that was used in a hammer fist type attack.

To read some accounts today, you'd think there were hordes of lads wielding these in an unstoppable wave of thuggery. That wasn't the case. It's only useful for a couple of hits and, while not pleasant to be hit by, it's not the fight-ender that it came to be known as. Still, you might find it useful in a pinch. To try it, simply open a newspaper, and roll up from top to bottom, then fold it in half. You can also reinforce it with masking tape if you like.

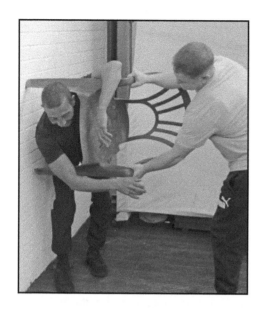

with the weight and balance. Obviously, chairs come in different shapes and sizes, so bear this in mind. A plastic chair might have less impact than a heavy wooden one, but is easier to manipulate. A bar stool is less of a shield, but has longer legs, so more distance and leverage.

Next, start working with a partner. At first, see how you can use the chair to keep them at bay. Or, explore how you can push them into a wall with it. Add in a knife to explore using the chair as a literal shield. See how you can jab to soft target areas with the legs..

A more useful and far more common item is the humble chair or stool. We've already covered working from a chair, but how about working *with* one? A solid chair makes a good obstacle to buy you some time. Or you can pick up the chair to throw it or use as a shield.

The obvious thing for the other person to do is grab the leg of the chair. This is good, this is what you want! Have your partner grab the chair. Then loop one leg over their elbow. With a little practice you will see how easy it is to lock the arm from this position. Plus the chair gives you a huge amount of leverage, so take care as you stretch the person out and take them to the floor.

Go back to our chair movement. Sit, wrap a foot around one leg as before. As you stand, grab the back of the chair in one hand and flick it up with your foot, a quick way to stand and have the chair ready.

Once you have it, move the chair around in your hands. As before, familiarise yourself

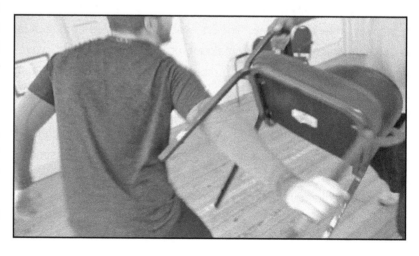

You can also work a takedown from the body. Push the chair into the attacker's hips, then twist and push the chair legs to the floor. As long as you have control of the hips, the rest of the body will follow.

MISSILE

Any object that can be picked up can be thrown, again the point is what will throwing it achieve? A heavy object like a brick can cause damage but, for the most part, we throw something as a distraction, to get a flinch that we can take advantage of. Think about what you regularly carry on your person. A handful of coins can be thrown into the face quite easily. Any sand, dirt, pebbles, etc to hand can be used in the same way.

Items of clothing may also be used. Imagine we are in a robbery scenario and we are wearing a baseball cap. Raise your hands up as if in surrender. Bring one or both hand to your head and slip a finger under the rim of the hat. Now, with a sharp flick of the wrist, launch the hat into your attacker's face. It won't cause any damage, but it will likely elicit a flinch response. The same works with sunglasses - though perhaps not an expensive pair! Raise your hands, then place

this will likely fall under the heading of an offensive weapon, particularly if prior intent can be proven.

If you are in the UK, then check that items have a *Secured by Design* accreditation, then you can be sure you are getting a decent product. One recently released useful item here is a sonic alarm that also sprays a DNA marker that can be used to ID an attacker.

two fingers at your temple and flick the glasses forward.

Heavier objects, such as our earlier book, are obvious missiles, though be aware that you are also, in effect, giving the object to your attacker! They may be used to create a flinch again, or perhaps to discourage pursuit.

The local police have been using these to great effect against motorbike joy riders. Rather than attempt a risky grab as the criminal rides past, the officer simply sprays, then visits and arrests later!

Of course, just having the alarm on you is no use, you need to know how to deploy it quickly. So either get used to carrying it your hand in potential trouble spots, or practice getting it out quickly. Keep it somewhere accessible, not in the depths of a bag.

There is another item which loosely comes under the missile, or projectile heading, and that is the personal alarm. These aren't really improvised weapons as such, as they are designed for a specific purpose, but can be very useful. There are many types available, from pepper sprays to sonic alarms.

Be sure to check the law in your area, as sprays may not be legal in some. A small can of perfume of hairspray usually is though. It was not uncommon at one time, for certain types to carry a small Jif lemon squeeze bottle filled with ammonia, though

CLOTHING

We will finish this chapter with a look at something that is present in almost every fight - unless you are attacked in a shower, perhaps - and that is clothing. There are two aspects to his work - how we can use our own clothing to help us, and how we can use another person's to hinder them. Let's start with that first.

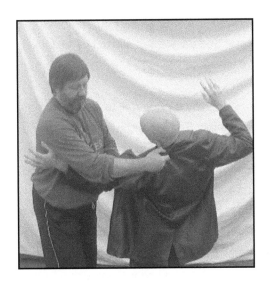

Clothing obviously gives us a very strong handle with which to manipulate people. So, step one, get your partner to put on an old jacket and start pulling them around. Bear in mind the takedown principles, look to break structure and work against the base and balance points. Also look at how you grip the jacket. As any good Judo player will tell you, curl your fingers into the grip. It's a bit like forming a fist as you grab, don't just grip the surface, you want a deep grip into the cloth. This is also what we term *grabbing the whole person.*

When you move, move deep. Don't just think about pulling the sleeve, pull the whole person. There are obvious points to work from. The collar, the sleeves, the bottom of the jacket. Sometimes, you can reinforce your movement. For

example, pull the bottom of the jacket out, place your knee inside it and use that to pull down (remember to work from the hip.)

You can get a simple and quick takedown from the collar. Grab one lapel and pull across towards the opposite shoulder. Grab the other lapel and lift up, across and then sharply down. With a little practice, this takes a person down in a second.

Another method is to use the clothing to impede the other person. Pull a hood over the head, or, if the jacket is open, pull the shoulders halfway down the arms to pin them in place.

Don't stop at the jacket. A tug on the outside of trousers can pull the hips out of line. Lifting the waistline sharply up and forward will help move a person (yes, the wedgie!) Even a t-shirt can be used - pull on the collar, then as the person moves forward, jab in and down to the throat.

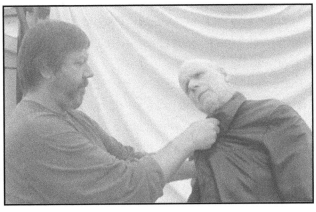

In short, explore all aspects of the clothing available. Items such as a hood, toggles, or scarf can be used to choke. Simply pull them sharply across the windpipe, at the same time break the structure to increase the effect.

Next, look at how to use your own clothing. The first step is to see how quickly you can remove a jacket. Inhale, hold your jacket, then exhale and take it off quickly. Repeat while moving. Finally, repeat as you fall to the floor.

There are a few reasons to do this work. One, we can get the jacket off quickly in order to use it. Two, we may be in a position where we need to change our appearance, to switch jackets with a friend. Three, the jacket may be on fire or have a hazardous material on it. Four, if someone has grabbed us, we can slip out of the jacket and escape

This is actually a good drill to repeat with all your clothing. For a real challenge, see if you can get out of a t-shirt without using your hands! This type of work helps develop good internal movement.

Next, have your partner grab your jacket and see how quickly you can escape from it. You then have the option of working back or creating distance. Obviously, you don't want to do this if you have your wallet, keys and phone in the pocket, so think again about how you carry your personal belongings, particularly if you are going into a potentially dangerous situation.

USING CLOTHING

Now we have the jacket off, how to use it? In many ways we go back to our work with a belt. We can use the jacket to wrap an arm. Have your partner feed in grabs or strikes and work as we did with the belt.

It may be that you wrap around the arm,

attacker's face. Again, it is not a powerful movement but it buys you some time.

especially against a grab. Against a punch, you may find it easier to throw the jacket over the fist, then grab and wrap from there.

Remember, you can also work against the legs - swing the jacket around the calf lift it to knee height and pull. This can work particularly well from the seated position. Also think about how you carry clothing. A jacket that is slung casually over a shoulder can easily be swung or thrown into an

The key, then, to working with any type of item or object is to understand its characteristics and how they can best be utilised in the moment.

Again, I emphasise, make sure you don't become psychologically attached to the item and put the training time in to play around with all these various objects, and any others you have to hand. Remember, everything is a weapon!

CHAPTER TEN
THE TEN POINTS OF SPARRING

We now have some strategies, some basic techniques, and some drill ideas. But how do we being to formulate all this into an integrated training program? How do we develop our skills beyond working the usual set routine of A does this, and B does that?

I once saw the question "how can they call it the System when there is no system?" For me this highlights one of the major differences between Systema and the more typical martial arts . They are seen (rightly or wrongly) as codified sets of movement which encapsulate the fighting methods developed by a particular person or family. Each has it's own idiosyncrasies - one might focus on short range work, one might involve large open movements, or a certain stance or hand formation.

Systema is less clear. There are no kata or set routines, work tends to be "of the moment". I can understand how a traditionalist would see this as unstructured. Looking beyond the surface, however, reveals something quite different.

First, let us not forget that Systema is the result of an accumulation of theory, practice and combat applications from previous generations. We should not forget the intense methods of development and testing that have gone into its formation, we do indeed stand "on the shoulders of giants".

Second, the system we work with is not a set of particular techniques, the system is the person themselves. We are composed of several systems, including nervous, respiratory, circulatory, bone, muscle, psychological, emotional. Further to that we live and operate within systems - school, society, religion, family and so on.

Systema then, as I see it, is the study first of our own systems and how they function in different situations. We then study how our systems interact with other people's. From there, we can explore how our systems interact with the wider "world systems." So, in answer to the original question - the system is all around us, but we often lose sight of that, much like a fish being unaware of the water.

This approach is principle led and so widens training out to cover anything you can think of, and plenty of things you can't think of! This is great, but it does pose the question asked at the start of the chapter.

One answer is to incorporate sparring into our training. The dictionary definition of sparring is " to make the motions of boxing without landing heavy blows, as a form of training." It may be derived from the Old English *sperran*, to "strike out". The most common view of sparring is from the sporting context. Wikipedia describes it as "essentially relatively free-form fighting, with enough rules, customs, or agreements to make injuries unlikely."

point, partly through resources and partly due to safety factors. Of course, resources can be stretched and with a certain outlook you realise the potential in almost any object or environment for training - the world is our gym!

With intensity come the question of compliance. We shall talk about this more later on, but the degree of compliance depends on the purpose of the drill - and we should never lose site of that purpose. It is very easy to step outside of the drill boundaries in order to "win". This achieves nothing. *The aim of the drill is not to defeat the aim of the drill.* It is for all people involved to develop.

This doesn't mean you should always be "nice" to your partner. If the drill calls for it, you may have to hit them hard or put them in an uncomfortable place. But it is very important that this is done with the correct attitude - one of learning and mutual growth rather than domination and abuse. In short leave the ego at the door, you will learn so much more.

You will probably find that in most Systema classes the majority of time is spent in these "sparring drills." Aside from some solo exercises, or breath work, virtually everything is done with at least one partner and with contact. However, these are not set drills, or choreographed attack / defence

For the purpose of this book I am widening the definition a little to include any two or more person training method that involves some element of self defence / combatives and is mostly freestyle in nature.

When training we should always bear three points in mind. The first is to always train with an eye to the safety of our partners and ourselves. It makes no sense to train self defence in such a way that causes psychological or physical damage to ourselves or others.

The second point is that training should be practical - it should bring something to the table in terms of increasing a skill, developing an attribute, understanding and so on.

The third point is that no matter how intense a drill may be, it is still *just training*. We can only replicate real life to a certain routines, they are almost always freestyle, within the parameters of the exercise. But how do we create these drills, how do we modify them as required?

One way I have found helpful is to think of the variables, or "points" which can be applied to any drill. I've named these the Ten Points of Sparring. This gives a framework on which to build your training. These variables are universal - it doesn't even matter which style or art you train in, this template can be applied and adapted to your own requirements.

We will now run through and explain these ten points, and give you some quick drill ideas to illustrate and help understand each point. You will see cross-over in some of our earlier drills, no doubt. As before, the drills described are starting points from which you can develop your own ideas - they are not finite in themselves. They should not be taken as any kind of syllabus and represent just one method of teaching or setting up drills. A drill is nothing more than a particular set of circumstances that will develop the skills of the people involved, they are not set in stone.

A great advantage of this approach is that through adjusting these variables, we can run the same drill at different levels of intensity, and so can include everyone in training. We try and avoid separating people, we prefer everyone to train together, this is one way to achieve that. I'd also like to mention that here I'm designating people as A, B, C etc, as we tend not to work with the "attacker / defender" or "uke/nage" model. We prefer that both people are getting benefit from a drill, rather than just being an "attack dummy."

Finally, be aware that drills can be layered - there can be several purposes contained within one drill, several "systems" being worked on at once. This means that people can get different benefits while working the same drill. So, let's run through the Ten Points of Sparring.

POINT ONE - SPEED

Speed is a simple variable to understand. You can walk very slowly, you can jog, you can sprint. In sparring terms it means regulating the speed at which we move, punch, grapple, etc. Usually, we will match speeds for everyone involved in the drill, but occasionally you can mix speeds up for an extra challenge.

Let's look at working slow first. It is often overlooked, but slow sparring is a very useful tool for skill development. Let's assume we are working with and against strikes. We may set the speed at around a quarter of normal speed – so it looks like we are working in slow motion. However, this doesn't mean we work "limp," it is important to maintain the same level of intent as if we were working fast. This allows us to start reading our partner's body language.

See, for example, how a person lifts the shoulder before throwing a jab. Working at slow speed takes a lot of the fear away, giving us a little thinking time to work out the best response. The same applies both visually and on a tactile level – the brain /body has time to feel and respond to contact. So we start to develop the ability to pre-empt a movement and the ability to take in and process information at a faster rate. Because as you increase speed, you will find you are still taking in the same amount of information that you were slowly.

The biggest challenge in working slow is to maintain a constant speed. If fear takes over, or if we see a chance opening, we may suddenly speed up to escape or to hit our partner. This tends to be contagious, as one person speeds up, so does the other. Fear and tension spread very quickly if we are not careful.

The single most effective way to control our speed is through breathing. After all speed tends to be a function of the nervous system, which in turn can be regulated most effectively through the breath. At a basic level, try this:

Inhale for a count of two. Hold for a couple of seconds. Exhale on the same count. Hold for a couple of seconds.

This is a basic "square breathing" pattern. Practice it as you walk or jog. Start with a 2 count and build up to 10, then back down again. You will soon learn to extend your breathing over the physical activity. In turn you will find your psyche remains calm, you are mentally focused and your endurance will increase. To control your speed, maintain a comfortable square breathing pattern as you spar.

DRILLS

1. SLOW BOXING
Two or more
Both partners moving and throwing/ countering strikes. Both work a square breathing pattern, let's say a four count. As you are working, focus in the inhale, 2, 3 4... exhale, 2, 3, 4. You should find that

maintaining the breathing will maintain the movement speed. This will work with three, four, or even a large group working en masse. You can of course add in kicks, grabs and so on. In order to increase the speed, quicken the breathing

2. BURST BREATHING
Two people
A walks towards B in a single, straight line. On the approach, B inhales, then exhales and moves to avoid A. Repeat. Start with a slow walk / slow inhale exhale. Gradually accelerate until A is running at B. By now B's exhale should be a quick burst

3. DON'T TOUCH!
Group
The whole group walks slowly within a confined space. The aim is to keep moving but avoid contact with anyone else. Gradually accelerate – from slow walk to jog to sprint. For extra pressure, reduce the work space.

WATCH OUT FOR

- beware of sudden acceleration

- keep your movements "real," don't do slow what you can't do fast

- try things out, explore your full range of movement

- vary the speed, don't work one speed every time

- tie your breathing in with your movement

- use slow work as an analytical tool, not just as an "easy drill"

POINT TWO - DISTANCE

Range is most important factor of any weapon. A good understanding of range is important, so too of course are position, angles and relative distance. Timing is a key concept in fighting and can help overcome many advantages an attacker may have.

Distance is an easy variable to put into place. Generally speaking the greater the distance the more time we have to react and so the easier things are. When we feel under pressure we tend to try and create more distance between ourselves and our partner. This becomes

most obvious in some types of sparring, where, even with protective gear, people stay just out of hitting range, then jump in and out with a quick jab or strike.

It is okay to work at this extended range, but there needs to be a good reason for it. One reason is to help people acclimatise to an attack. Working at a distance gives the person a clear visual line of attack and some time to avoid it. This begins to teach them about angles of attack and the best positions to move to.

On the other hand, we can also start work up very close - for example with a knife actually contacting the body. This helps people get accustomed to the feel of a metal knife and, when the point is pushed into the body, helps develop tactile

sensitivity, awareness and reaction against a stab. This may form part of a disarming technique, or it may be damage limitation if a stab does get through to the body. It is also a good drill to promote relaxation of the major muscle groups.

Other drills call for the range to change - the aim may be to learn how to close distance quickly. Distance drills do not necessarily have to be about avoidance, they can also be used for awareness and sensitivity training. For example, as we saw in a previous chapter, you have to remain at a close distance and follow / copy another person's movements. This can be further complicated by having someone simultaneously copy your movements. This type of training is very good for developing reactions, free movement and the ability to "read" and pre-empt someone else's moves.

If we are working to maintain a set distance, we of course primarily work visually. However we can add in tactile elements too. The partners might have a stick or a ball placed between them, which they have to not let fall. You can use a rope or scarf tied to each partner's wrist or ankle in order to stop them moving apart.

Another option is to work from physical contact. It can be a

168

challenge doing even the basic exercises while maintaining "back to back" or "shoulder to shoulder" with one or more others.

DRILLS

1. STICK EVASION
Two people
A wields the stick. B must stay at extended range and avoid contact with the stick. After this, B must avoid the stick but move in to close/touching range of A. Strikes / takedowns can be added in.

2. STICKY IN THE MIDDLE
Group
A stays in the centre of the training area and wields the stick. The rest of the group must avoid contact with the stick. They must also try and work in to tap A on the shoulder. If touched with the stick they immediately retreat to the edge of the area. If they tap the shoulder, they switch positions and become A

3. CLOSE IN BOXING
Two people
A steps on B's foot to keep B in place and feeds in strikes. B moves / deflects the strikes. Change roles. Then both partners attack and defend simultaneously

4. KNIFE DRILL DISTANCE
Two people
A with knife feeds clear, large attacks from a distance of six feet or so. B is to avoid the attacks with stepping, body movement and/or arm deflection

5. KNIFE DRILL CLOSE
Two people
A with knife pushes the point slowly into B's body. B responds by softly moving the body away from the point and trying to keep the flat of the blade against the body. B works to stay on the spot and not step away.

WATCH OUT FOR

- be careful to stay within the training zone / distance set for the drill

- use as many senses as possible when judging distance, sight, touch sound

- use distance to explore drawing/blocking the draw with weapons

- if people are uncomfortable at a certain

distance, make them work it, but slowly at first

- don't forget the breathing!

POINT THREE - CONTACT

Levels of contact can range from none at all through to landing a strike as hard as you can. The norm tends to be somewhere in between. As a rule we prefer to always work with some contact. There are several important reasons for this:

- it helps with range

- it overcomes psychological issues of hitting and being hit

- you get used to the idea that in a fight you might get hit!

- it gives an opportunity to practice breathing and control of our psyche

- it helps develop good striking ability as opposed to always "pulling" a strike

- we learn how to gauge our hits and work at different depths of strike, we get instant feedback

Obviously, safety is a major factor - heavier contact should only be carried out once people have the mechanisms in place to deal with it. The better people are at taking hits, the heavier the hits can become. Of course there are always some areas which will be off-limits as far as power shots are concerned, unless perhaps we are using protective gear (see later on).

But even at a basic level it is important that there be at least "touch" contact. A very good method when working at this stage is to use the fist to push rather than to strike. This doesn't hurt anyone but gives valuable feedback concerning angles and positions of the strike.

Contact does not necessarily have to be related to speed. It is possible to work quite slow but with heavy strikes. Likewise, with the right kind of control, we should be able to work fast but give only surface hits. One tip to help with this is to keep the fists quite relaxed, this way we will not hit too deeply.

Contact and non-contact work can be mixed into one drill. A simple idea is for one person to try and touch the other with a stick. One is trying to get contact, the other to avoid it. I like to use gauntlet drills for this kind of work (see below).

Another element with this variable is the idea of non-contact work. This has always been a controversial area in martial arts, particularly when it comes with claims of mysterious masters using "super-human" powers to affect others, sometimes in quite dramatic ways. That aside, the non-touch work I've experienced in Systema has always been explained clearly in psychological terms. At a basic level, we can think of this as eliciting a flinch response by putting an obstacle in the way. For example a clear flick towards the eyes or groin can affect a change in movement and structure in a person, which we can then take advantage of. This is a starting point and can lead into other areas of training, such as reading body language, affecting others through our own actions and so on.

I've always found this kind of work is actually easier to apply in real life than in training - because no-one knows what is supposed to happen, reactions are spontaneous and natural. I remember a new guy who asked me "can you really affect someone with no contact?". I glanced over his shoulder before answering. He turned his head to see what I was looking at and I said "No, not really". He never came back to training....

Alongside this is "soft work". This is where we try and influence someone with a minimum of contact. This is useful in that we learn to work with minimum tension on our part, and our work does not aggravate those we are working against, making it easier to gain compliance. There are numerous close protection drills that help develop this useful skill - one that I've used several times to calm down a situation. Most recently two guys were squaring up and I was able to quietly lead one off to the other side of the room and prevent a fight. Touch has a powerful effect on the nervous system, either to calm or agitate, so a study

of different contact levels is very important

DRILLS

1. EXCHANGING HITS
Two people
A stands slightly to the side of B and administers strikes. Change roles. Experiment with depth of strike to establish comfort levels. Following this you can work back and forward, exchanging hits. Try to let your body response to a strike power your own hit.

2. GAUNTLET
Group
Form two rows, with about six feet between each person. The rows face each other, everyone lined up to a gap opposite.

Everyone has a stick which they can, at first, hold in a static position. The drill is for a person to go down the middle of the row avoiding contact with the sticks. After a while, the people with the sticks can make a single repetitive movement - say a back and forth lunge. Once again the person has to go down the middle avoiding contact. For a real challenge add random stick movements, increase the speed, etc

3. SOFT TOUCH / NON-CONTACT
Three people

A has to walk up and initiate some form of contact with B, a handshake, touch the shoulder, etc. C has to prevent this by quietly re-directing A. This may be done by lightly pushing the hip or shoulder. It might be done by presenting a barrier to A, then deflecting him in another direction with a gesture. It could be a flick to the eyes or groin in order to elicit a flinch response, followed by some re-direction. However it is done, it should be done lightly and with minimum show.

WATCH OUT FOR

- don't hit heavy out of fear or tension, monitor your psyche

- always hit your partner with care, not hate or aggression

- get comfortable with all types of contact

- if contact levels are too high, bring them back down

- be open to exploring light and non-contact work

- don't lose sight of reality or imagine you have super powers!

- as always, breathing.... when you hit, when you get hit, and for everything else in-between!

POINT FOUR - TECHNIQUE

Sometimes we will practice one specific technique, either in order to explore a principle, or where some technical knowledge is required. A good example would be applying a rear naked choke.

Another approach is to practice a specific group of techniques - for example arm/wrist locks. This allows us to concentrate solely on one particular area in order to develop skills in it. The obvious thing then, is that both people stay "on track" during the drill.

I always use the example (which actually happened) of working against the wrist and fingers. This was a first time for most of the group, so we were working from contact in order to get the mechanics down. All except for one guy. He tucked his hands under his armpits and kept moving away from his partner. It was gently pointed out that no-one would learn how to apply wrist locks in this way, but he seemed set on "winning" the drill. I've heard this described as *throwing dirt into the honey*, we have some other phrases for it too....

To turn things around, we may wish to learn more about defence from a certain technique. So we set up our partner to feed in only kicks, or grabs and so on. This gives us a chance to repeatedly experience something and so learn a good response against it

DRILLS

1. CHOKES

Two people

A stands, sits, or lays down while B carefully applies a choke hold. The hold should be put on until A taps, when they are immediately released.

Repeat the drill again, this time A works to escape the hold.

Repeat again, this time A works to escape, then immediately applies a choke to B, who escapes and applies a choke, repeat and continue

2. KICKS

Five people

A stands in the centre, the rest of the group surround him at kicking range. A has to smoothly kick each of the group, without bringing the foot back to the floor

3. THE HOOK

Two people

A is only allowed to feed in hook punches. B must try as many different responses as possible to the hook. Try taking the punch, blocking at, jamming the arm, evading, deflecting, ducking and so on. Repeat with any other type of punch or kick

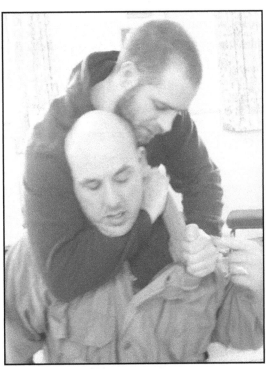

WATCH OUT FOR

- make sure everyone understands the limits of the drill

- if the drill calls for it, allow your partner to work

- once comfortable with one technique, add in variations

- think of this as a lab, experiment!

- when working chokes always be aware of partner safety, release immediately on tap.

POINT FIVE - COMPLIANCE

Outside people are often surprised at the amount of compliance in martial arts training. They seem to think all our time is spent fighting in some sort of gladiatorial trial and that training is all about being "hard" or "tough". The reality is far different of course, in every style or method there is a considerable amount of development work prior to any kind of full contact. This

is no different to any other area of life or training. No musician plays their first gig at Wembley Arena in front of thousands of people - and if that did happen, they would be so out of their depth as to be useless. More importantly they would be unlikely to gain anything from the experience, indeed it could put them off for life!

Having said that, there is the opposite extreme, where everything you do in training works and classmates obligingly crumple at a touch. Once again, the truth lies somewhere in-between. So how much should we resist what our partner is doing? That depends entirely on the purpose of the drill. We have already spoken about the wristlock situation above- but that is purely to learn the actual mechanics of the lock. At some point we need to know what to do if your partner resists. There are three aspects to consider when it comes to compliance.

The first is tension as resistance - our partner grabs and we can apply a lot of tension in order to counter the technique

The second is to not let the partner apply their technique in the first place, ie to be evasive

The third is to actively work back against our partner, so maybe while they are grabbing us, we punch them

Once you have these three ideas in mind it becomes easy to start grading levels of resistance. There are just two other things to consider – one is the relative level of each partner. If a person is highly skilled they may be able to stop their partner very easily. This can prove frustrating for the beginner. A good person can adjust on the fly in order to give their partner a good training experience.

The second consideration is safety. If you have a joint put under pressure, you may be able to apply tension in order to stop it moving. However this may then give your partner a quandary – do they apply more power in order to drive their technique through, if in doing so they may damage the joint?

Sometimes what looks like compliance is, in fact, self preservation. A person is moving, rolling or similar in order to protect themselves from their partner's technique. This partly goes back to what I said before about the better you can deal with impact, etc, the more intensely you can work.

It also goes back to my earlier point about the notion of the *uke/nage* model not being applicable to our method. A short example – in my earlier days I was quite used to being one of the training dummies used by the teacher in order to illustrate a technique. My role was quite clear – punch clearly at the signified target, then stay still and accept whatever came back. That's how things were!

The first time I trained with Mikhail I got a shock. He asked me to attack so I duly threw out a punch and stood still. He let me do this a couple of times, but looked a bit puzzled. The third time he gave me such a crack on the jaw that I did the most perfect twist, fall and roll I ever did in my life! He explained he did this because he wanted me to move – this process was not solely about him showing his moves against my attack, but also an opportunity for me to learn how to move against his counter attack. It was a powerful lesson.

It's an extremely important idea and one that forms the basis for a lot of the online miscomprehension of Systema video clips. People assume that the person hitting is "showing off" his punches and the other partner is just a dummy. In fact, these type of drills are often far more for the benefit of the person being hit, thrown, or whatever else is going on.

A good instructor should feel there is nothing to prove and in any case showing off

against a static dummy proves nothing.

Another point is about understanding what is actually happening to you. I have seen people so wrapped up in their "resistance" and tension in training they failed even to feel a training knife being poked into their back by a third partner. I've seen people "fight through" having fingers placed on their eyes, a hand on the throat or a light strike to a vulnerable area. It doesn't mean you have to fade at the first touch, but you must acknowledge at least the potential of what is going on. This is about self awareness as much as anything else.

There is a psychological aspect to resistance, too. Training that is always done in a cool, calm, friendly environment is not necessarily preparing us for real life. People can be belligerent, aggressive, insulting, they may shout and scream at us, even if no physical harm is intended. This can have as dramatic an effect on our nervous system as any punch or kick, so it

is good to cover this in training too, particularly when we get into scenario work.

Resistance levels, then, should be set according to the purposes of the drill and the relative skills of the people involved. I find that my regular guys, who have worked together for years, are able to go at high speed and resistance levels without any problems. We are fortunate to have had very few injuries in training over the years and I can say that those few we have had were down to people going outside of the drill boundaries.

DRILLS

1. HOLD THE KNIFE
Two people
A holds a training knife in outstretched hand. The grip is fairly loose and the hand is static. B works to take the knife from the grip.
First, A offers no resistance. Then A offers part tension, full tension and, finally tension and movement to prevent B taking the knife.

2. TAKEDOWNS
Two people
A approaches B, who initiates a takedown. Before contact A immediately drops to the floor. Repeat with variations
  − A drops on first touch
  − A is neutral, so the takedown will only work if done correctly
  − A passively tries to prevent the takedown

with tension

- A tries to prevent the takedown with soft, evasive movement
- A goes with the takedown and reverses it
- A resists the takedown and reverses it
- A does everything they can (within safety limits) to prevent the takedown.

3. GRAPPLING

Two people

Partners sit back to back. At the signal "go" A works at an intense level, B can only passively resist , ie use structure / softness to nullify A's work. Repeat, adding in more active resistance each time. Switch and repeat. Finally, both partners attack and defend at full resistance

4. KEEP CALM!

Two people

A has to remain calm and in control of breathing while B is verbally aggressive and abusive. There doesn't have to be physical contact but B should try and get A annoyed, upset, fearful, etc.

WATCH OUT FOR

- ensure resistance levels are set and understood before the drill

- watch out for fear-based tension or resistance

- don't take advantage of the situation in order to injure or hurt your partner

- be prepared to experiment with different levels of resistance

- don't be concerned about giving up ground or "losing face", the aim is to survive not "win"

- be aware as to what is going on and take care of vulnerable areas

- be sure to monitor levels of emotional tension

- for challenging areas of work, particularly psychological, put a "safe word" in place that will immediately end the drill if spoken

POINT SIX - ENVIRONMENT

Environment is such an obvious variable, yet so many people train week after week in exactly the same room, they may even stand in exactly the same space and work with

exactly the same people. One of the first comments about our classes is…. "there's no mats!"

There are a few reasons for this. The most obvious is that 99.999% of the world is not matted – and that is where things happen. Groundwork on a normal floor gives us much better feedback and means our bodies learn to relax so much quicker. Of course, it is uncomfortable at first, but discomfort can be a good teacher! Likewise learning to fall and dive on a normal surface teaches us good technique very quickly. This means we can adapt much easier to whatever surface we are working on.

Don't think that you should never use mats, though. There may be some circumstances with newer or very nervous people or if you are trying more daring falls, where mats can help at first. But they should be removed at the earliest opportunity so that they don't become a habit.

Whilst on the subject of ground surface, even if people don't train with mats, they tend to be on a nice wooden floor. Even working on a flat lawn can make a big difference, let alone uneven ground.

In short, vary your training space. Get outside, onto grass, concrete, woodland, anywhere and everywhere. Now, this does open a question as to the viability of training outside in the UK. I find that even training "normal" exercise outside attracts attention here - whereas in the Far East public spaces are full of people training everything from Tai Chi to ballroom dancing. So you have to pick your spots carefully.

Our Leicester group train in a park and on their first session had the police swing by to investigate reports of a "big fight" going on! Testament to the training perhaps and it was all resolved, but it bears consideration, especially if you are thinking of using training weapons. If you are not in a public space, make sure you get permission from the land owner. Unless you want to run an evasion drill as we once did in a park after closing time.....

There are many types of environment to work in – a car or vehicle of some kind, narrow corridor, different rooms, stairs and so on. We are lucky in that our regular hall has stairs, a kitchen, toilets, a car park, a stage - within one place we have a good variation of training spaces.

Environment can also cover sound (try training with different types and volumes of music). It can refer to the number of people around. If you have a large group, put them in a small room and get them to move through and around, or work group sparring. Look back to the crowd drills, don't just think "fighting", any of these drills may help if you are somewhere and there is an emergency situation. Remember Systema training is for survival, not just for a fight!

DRILLS

1. CAR MOVEMENT
Spend some time moving in and around your car. Enter and exit through different doors, Go in and out of the windows. Move from front seat to back. See how you can use the car as cover or a barrier

2. WORKING THE DOOR

Two or more people
A stands in the doorway and attempts to stop B getting through. A obviously has to work within the confines of the space, they cannot move out from the doorway.

3. FURNITURE
Group
Fill your training space with chairs, tables and similar objects. Navigate slowly and at speed, standing and on the ground. Try different light levels or eyes closed. Practice fighting in the same space, in pairs or groups

4. A WALK IN THE WOODS
Group
Run your usual partner /group drills outdoors, in woods or forest. See how the uneven ground affects balance but also look for opportunities to use the environment to help you.

4. WATER, WATER
Group
Training in water can be very challenging, from both a physical and psychological point of view. As a start we suggest doing regular exercises in different depths of water, then trying regular two person work. Of course there is also ample opportunity for breath holds!

WATCH OUT FOR

- be aware of safety issues, whether it's ground conditions or sharp corners on

objects

- be aware of on-lookers and potential interruptions

- don't wait for the weather, if it ain't raining it ain't training!

- practice this at home. You should be able to move smoothly in and around your property in all conditions

- look at objects not just as obstacles but as training opportunities, you can do pull ups on tree branches, use benches to roll on, etc

- water work should always be carefully supervised with relevant safety procedures in place

POINT SEVEN - RESTRICTION

Adding restriction to a sparring drill is usually done for two reasons. It can be to simulate a situation where you are not fully functional due to injury, are carrying something or are restricted due to environment. It can also be in order to focus on a specific sense or area of the body.

Restriction is most simply done by taking one or more parts of the body out of the equation. So you might work with hands in pockets, standing on one leg, carrying some object, having to work on the spot and so on. Blindfold work is extremely useful. It develops tactile sensitivity,

general awareness, intuitive feeling and is good for fear control. Group blindfold exercises also teach teamwork, trust and communication skills

There are other aspects to working with restriction. There may be a situation where it is not appropriate for you to hit someone , so you have to work within the restriction of trying to restrain them only. Restriction can also apply to time - giving a drill a specific length can be useful in some cases, especially testing or task related drills.

DRILLS

1. BLINDFOLD PAIRS
Two people
A is blindfolded. B slowly approaches and pushes A from different directions. A must go with the movement, to the ground if necessary. Following this, B can lightly strike

or kick. A must respond with movement and can also add in a hold /takedown response

2. BLINDFOLD GROUP

Four or more

A is blindfolded and put in the centre of the group. Each member of the group takes turns to attack A with a push, grab, strike, etc. A must respond as best they can. Intensity can vary from slow attacks at regular intervals to faster with little or no gap in-between.

3. DON'T SPILL IT!

Group

A must walk through the group whilst carrying an object. In the past we have used a medicine ball (to simulate a baby), a tray of drinks (water, not beer!) and other items. The drill can start slowly, then faster movement and or offensive / defensive actions added in

4. AAAARGH JIM LAD!

Group

This one comes out of an incident at Vladimir's class. A regular student turned up with his leg in plaster following an accident, saying he couldn't train but wanted to come along anyway to watch. Vladimir said the guy could train and got everyone else in the class to place a long stick down one pant leg in order to even the playing field! So you can do regular exercises, drills, etc, with this or other such restrictions.

WATCH OUT FOR

- with blindfold work always have at least one sighted person keeping an eye on things

- when working against a restricted partner, attack them as required but no cheap shots

- injury can be an opportunity to explore different ways of training

- be aware of your own fear as a restriction, note how it can prevent you from trying new things

- be open to people of all abilities, training should be such that it can be adapted to almost any condition.

POINT EIGHT - EQUIPMENT

Equipment can refer to regular sparring gear – gloves, head guards, padding, gum shields and so on. We have found there are pros and cons to using them. On the plus side, it allows for higher levels of speed and contact. On the down side we find it can restrict breathing and vision, allows a person to continue despite heavy hits (though headgear doesn't necessarily prevent concussive impact) and gives a different sense of distance if large gloves are worn.

Of course, you don't have to be totally covered. We sometime use light bag gloves as hand protection for faster sparring, which generally works well.

For some areas of training though, protective

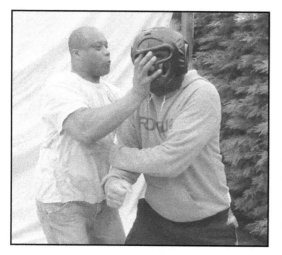

and power in their strikes.

Weapons are part of almost all martial arts training. There are numerous benefits to learning the use of and defence against all types of weapon, be it bladed, blunt or projectile. We can think of "proper" weapons, such as knife and also "improvised" weapons, everyday items that may be used in some way, such as a chair, items of clothing etc

gear is compulsory - for example, eye protection if using airsoft or fast weapons work. However we have found that this type of equipment has little or no effect on the actual work.

Equipment doesn't just mean protective gear though. Perhaps the single most useful bit of equipment for Systema training is a stick – it should be about 4' long and reasonable thick / strong. There are are huge amount of stick exercises for solo, partner and group work.

When it comes to exercise some people like to use sledgehammers, kettle-bells, an iron ball, logs, power bands and similar for training. Again this gives us the opportunity to be creative and not just think "gym weights" for training strength.

Something else we use are focus pads. Again, they have pros and cons but can be very useful for helping people develop flow

DRILLS

1. MILLING
Two people
Both partners have full padded gear on and can fight "all out" for a set period of time. The aim is not so much to win, but to remain psychologically strong throughout and not give up

2. WEAPONS FOR MOVEMENT
Group
Use a training weapon. Learn to move smoothly with the weapon, either in the hand or carried. Transition from standing to ground while deploying the weapon, move in different planes while wielding it. Once this is done, apply the movements against others in the group. This may mean pointing (with training gun or, under supervision, airsoft), slashing attacks with a blade, swinging a length of chain and so on. The aim is to learn movement with and against the weapon

3. MIX AND MATCH

Two people.

A and B choose the same or different weapon and work against each other. Stick vs knife, chain vs stick etc

4. IMPROVISED WEAPONS

Group

Have the group each bring three items from home. Swap the items around, then use them against various attacks. Improvised weapons can broadly be divided into flexible (belt, chain), blunt (book, chair), sharp (screwdriver, scissors), clothing and projectile (coins, gravel). Find the key principles of each and you then only have to adapt, rather than learn how to use each separately. This will also open you to the potential of any item to hand. Be aware of the strengths and weaknesses of any weapon too.

WATCH OUT FOR

- think "safety" when working with any weapon or object, particularly eye safety

- be creative, anything heavy is a weight, anything large can be climbed over, under or through

- don't get psychologically attached to any weapon, it is just a tool

- the weapon is only as effective as the person wielding it, it is not a substitute for good skills

POINT NINE - PURPOSE

It is absolutely vital in training that we are aware of why we do what we do. It is very easy to slip into a routine, particularly in some of the more "restricted" training approaches. I remember at my first school we did exactly the same exercise and warm up routine, week in week out, for years. It was never questioned, and people always stood in "their" spot.

I'm not one of those people who writes out weekly goals for myself, then ticks boxes off a checklist, but I do think it is important in at least some stages of training to have a clear goal and a method for getting there. Let us also not forget though, that there is the idea

of training for the training's sake – because it is enjoyable!

Another aspect to this is the question of balance. I've been in classes where one particular aspect of the training becomes (to my mind) over-emphasised. A prime example is the push-hands training we see in some styles. What begins as a useful exercise for developing tactile awareness, structure and technique becomes almost the whole point of the training.

The criteria for effectiveness then becomes how good you are at a particular drill rather than how well you can use the skills developed from it in real life. We should always understand the purpose of restrictions in training is not to just be able to work under those restrictions!

Of course, restriction forms the basis of any type of sport or competition and there is nothing wrong with that. A good knowledge of the rule set and how to work within it is vital. I'm not one for the old *streets vs sports* argument, it seems obvious to me that there is both cross-over in terms of skills and attributes and differences in terms of environment and consequences. The best people I've met in each field (and some who have done both) are well aware of that, in the same way that a top footballer would never claim to be a great gymnast, though both are at a peak of functional fitness relevant to their activities.

Training for a specific event or sport means we are able to focus our efforts towards that goal. The same goes for a person training for a particular role, such as a doorman. It is when we start training for "self defence" that things can become less clear. In any kind of sparring drill, then, it is important to have a clearly defined reason for the drill. I have divided these into seven categories:

PLAY
An enjoyable exchange between two or more people. While each may be working on skills, the main goal is simply to enjoy the movement and be "in the moment". It gives a chance to be creative and try out new ideas or movements in a relaxed environment. Psychologically it is good for us to "play" occasionally. It's an outlook we have as

children that is often lost in later life.

ATTRIBUTE DEVELOPMENT

We can think of a technical skill, such as playing a piano – but we need certain attributes in order to bring that skill to life – touch, feel, flow. The same applies to our training. Some of the attributes to consider are balance, visual awareness, tactile sensitivity, emotional awareness, flow, reactions, speed, team work, confidence, communication, fear management, co-ordination, fine and gross motor skills, health and so on.

LEARNING

The aim here is to learn or refine a new technical skill, or how to work with some piece of equipment. Work is restricted solely to the technique or skill in question

TESTING

Once we have some skills we need to test them. Trying to hit a moving opponent, testing movement skills against a weapon and so on. In each case there should be a clearly defined "succeed or fail" element built in so you can gauge how your skills held up!

PROBLEM SOLVING

Problem solving might be as simple as being put into an arm-bar, then working out how to escape from it. It might be how to move and protect a person through a group of attackers. Generally this type of drill will be run at less than full speed with plenty of time to work things out

TASK BASED

Similar to Problem Solving but in "real time". The task might be to pin a person to the floor for five seconds. Or it could be to prevent someone getting through a doorway, extracting someone from a car and so on. There will usually be a time limit in place to keep things focused.

SIMULATION

In essence this means creating some kind of scenario or role-play in order to simulate a real life situation. They can be very simple, or quite involved (as we will detail later on).

As we have done earlier in this book, it is good to take examples from actual

experience, either from the people in the group, or as seen on Youtube and the like. A basic example might be a simple robbery attempt, which could be set up something like this -

A walks through the training area. At some point B approaches, pulls a knife and demands B's wallet.

Even with a basic example there are all the existing variables to throw in, plus some other considerations. B can be quiet or verbally aggressive. A might stand and fight, run off, or give over the wallet – it is rare that there is one right answer. The scenario can be run several times to explore different approaches and outcomes

One problem when working scenarios is the question of "friends acting". When you know each other well it is not always easy to get a real fear feeling going, even with the best acting! We have got round this in the past by bringing in some outside people unknown to the group – so at one camp we ran, a cross country run was interrupted by two "angry farmers" to good effect! For regular work try mixing people around so they work with someone they don't know so well, that should help.

Scenario work also brings in the idea of pre, during and post incident considerations. There may be a build up to physical action, which gives a good opportunity to develop fear control. As we know, any physical action needs to be appropriate to the situation, or post-incident consequences may be dire. I see some schools practicing neck breaks and kicks to the head of a downed attacker. Appropriate in some cases perhaps, but in others you will be in the dock alongside your attacker. As emphasised throughout this book, sound knowledge of the local law is vital.

Likewise, we have the question of consequences that we spoke about in before. These are all points we can is work through and discuss via scenario training.

POINT TEN - INTENSITY

Our final variable is how we blend all the other variables together! They can and should be mixed and matched in almost countless ways in order to enhance the training experience. The best way to think of the variables is like a graphic equaliser - each band can be adjusted individually until the mix is just how you like it.

This brings a huge amount of variety into our training and helps prevent lessons becoming stale and too comfortable. The whole training session can even be built around the virtually the same drill run in a variety of ways. For example, start with knife handling, then go to close-in flow knife-disarming, build up speed to test, work in some problem solving with the knife held close in a restricted space, then finish with some scenario work based on some real life knife attack situations.

This method works best with a principle-led approach, but there is nothing to stop you using it for more technique-orientated work either. The important things are that everyone is aware of the drill boundaries and the purposes of the drill (and I often find we discover some other purposes as we go along) and that the drill is open to change and adaptation as and when necessary.

CHAPTER ELEVEN
TRAINING

We have covered the basic elements of self defence and some specific areas. For our final chapter we will look at ways to integrate all these methods into a cohesive training program, and also look at some refinements that we can add into our work.

Self defence courses typically run for six to ten sessions or so. Many are designed to give people some simple techniques to use in common types of dangerous situation. This is one approach, though, to me, one that misses out many of the vital factors present in an situation. It can give a false sense of security, where people come to rely on the "magic technique" rather than their own capabilities. There is no getting away from the fact that against a determined attacker, we need certain attributes to prevail, not just blindly flail with a fist that may well get broken if it meets hard bone.

Another consideration, when it comes to any type of training, is our personal health and well-being. I have seen many people damage their bodies through training for self defence - in some cases seriously. Think about the logic of that for a moment. You might do more damage to yourself than the single drunk attacker you might meet in your lifetime. While we must expect pain and discomfort during training, I have no time for Instructors who see inflicting or suffering damage as part of the process. Indeed, I have heard some even boast about this, about how "tough" their schools are because of the injuries caused to students. Aggression is almost invariably a mask for fear, so we can draw our own conclusions about that type of Instructor.

Military style training is, of a necessity, generally more concentrated than that of the average civilian. It is also tied in to a specific purpose. There is nothing wrong with adapting elements of that into our training - indeed, that is something we do in Systema. But always with an eye to our personal goals and situations and our own health and well-being, physical and psychological. I mention this because it is the foundation for how we organise and adapt our training. We should be very clear of our goals before we start. Bear in mind your own situation, likely events and time available to spend on training, then you can decide which particular areas you would like to prioritise.

If our aim is to teach others, we must also be aware of their goals and needs. They may also need to be tempered with realism. On the other hand, sometimes people will find they are capable of so much more than they thought. Always, the primary focus for me, with any person wishing to learn "everyday" self defence is awareness. And the root foundation of that is self awareness, in other words all our breathing, posture, tension and general health work.

Over the years I have taught dancers, special forces personnel, musicians, LEOs, the elderly, pretty much anyone you can think of. The first thing we cover is the same across the board - breath work. I highly recommend that you

start and end each training session with some form of breathing drill. It may be laying on the floor, static, or it could be incorporated into any of the core exercises. Whichever method, strengthening that mind-breath-body link will enhance all aspects of the training session.

From breath work we normally transition into exercise. That may be for movement, for strength, for posture or, ideally a combination. Quite often the exercise will be tuned into the theme of the class. Say we are working on ground fighting, for example, the exercises will likely involve. floor movement or various kinds. Following this, we move into drills of the sort detailed in previous chapters. These may be to develop attributes, to practice technical work, or to highlight specific skill sets.

Following that we run through our sparring or free play drills, which can range from slow work to play-fight to scenarios to full

testing. We finish with breathing, massage, or a mixture of the two and always close the session with a circle. We sit in a circle and each person makes comments about the class, or any other relevant topic.

That is roughly the class format I have been using for the past twenty years and I've found it works well. It is easily adaptable on the fly and allows everyone to train together. One other approach I tried when working with new people was devote a certain time - say a month - to a specific topic. So we would run four consecutive sessions on falls and rolls, or strikes, etc. That allowed everyone to quickly get up to speed in the basics. However, each of those sessions still always started with breathing and movement.

You can use the same format if you have no formal class but are training with friends. In that case, pick some of the drills that interest you the most from this book and work through them. Remember that these drills are not set in stone but are simply designed to create an environment or situation in which you can develop your skills and attributes. Of course there are also numerous other book and film resources available too. I'd also recommend getting in a Zoom class with Vladimir or Mikhail where you can. These days you don't even have to travel!

What about solo training? At times, we may not be able to join a class or group. As well as that, are there things we should be practicing on our own? In a word, yes! A lot of our breathing, movement, tension and awareness drills can be practiced alone. You should be putting at least a little time in each day to do some exercise, be it the core push-up, squat, sit ups, floor movement, working with a stick and so on. My book *Systema Solo Training* has plenty of ideas, and again there are numerous other resources available.

If you can do nothing else, then work your breathing. This can be done sitting at a desk and takes little time. On a wider level, observe your internal reaction to the events around you. Try to pinpoint moments when stress begins to take hold. It is much easier to manage tension at this point than later on.

When you do this I hope you will begin to realise how Systema practices infuses our everyday life and give us true "self defence." Not just what to do in a confrontation, but practical tools to deal with all the ups and downs of being a human being.

REFINEMENT

What I have presented so far in this book is what we might call basic or entry-level work. Having said that, I don't really like to classify work as basic or advanced, as it carries some connotations - for me, at least!

A lot of martial art styles have the concept of progression and rank. We start at a

certain grade and as we learn more of the syllabus, we progress up the ranks. This may be fairly informal or it may even be the case that grades never mix - even to the extent that each grade has to stand in a certain spot in the training hall. This brings in the idea that certain

aspects of the syllabus or certain moves or techniques are "advanced" even to the point of being secret and shown only to a select few disciples.

Yet how advanced can a movement be? A movement can certainly be more acrobatic and demanding to perform. But does that relate to a practical use, or is it just a flashy movement? Again, from a practical level, isn't it better to be simple and direct than try to carry out a complex set of techniques that you have learned in a fixed pattern?

Here's a prime example. A while back was teaching a young family, Mum, Dad and their three young boys. We ran the grab-evade drill for the first time, where the aim is to move away from and evade the grabs

of your training partners. I gave the instructions, "Don't let the people grab you!" The adults began bouncing around, using jerky movement to try and dodge a grab, becoming very tense both physically and mentally. Not so the kids. In the corner of the hall was a stack of tables, about four deep. Without any conference, the kids all immediately ran into the corner, under the tables, unreachable in their little cave. Beautiful.

So, rather than use the word "advanced", I prefer to say "refined." We can apply this to any activity. Take running - we can run with our arms flailing, stomping heavily on the ground, or we can run like a cross-country runner, smoothly, efficiently, able to cover long distances with no trouble. It is the same activity and movement - left foot, right foot - but one is more refined.

When we first begin Systema, particularly if new to training, we find our movements are a little jerky, we may struggle against tension, and lack flow and co-ordination. As we progress, our movements will become "cleaner." Not just physically, but psychologically, too.

Vladimir's brother Valentin Vasiliev once explained this to me very nicely. To paraphrase he said, image we are attacked and we fight our attacker off and escape. Our actions may be identical but what changes is how clean our work is. At one level our movements may be more crude,

outwards - where are my hands and feet, what is the other person doing, and so on. That is a good place to start but once we have a sound grasp of the basics we should begin to work more internally.

Here is a simple drill that will give you a good start point. First of all, do some solo squats, but in a particular way. Stand and inhale, bring some tension into your legs and hips. Exhale and release that tension, so dropping down into the squat. To lift, inhale and image being pulled up from the crown of the head as your chest expands. In other words, we are trying not to engage the thigh muscles so much, but use this feeling of relax inside / fall   expand inside / raise to carry out the squat. This is internal work.

we use more tension than we need, our mindset is agitated, fearful and aggressive. When the situation is over, we still carry those things with us. This is what creates PTSD, particularly if repeated often.

Instead, we are looking to carry out our work as smoothly, quickly and effectively as possible, without allowing that fear and tension to get its hooks into us. This way, when we move away from the situation we feel "cleaner."

This refinement is an on-going process, we never reach the end. When we look at the more subtle work demonstrated by the top teachers, we begin to see just how deep this process can go. But how do we begin it? The answer is by looking inwards.

Typically, when we work against another person, our attention is directed

Next, stand back to back with a partner, with just one point of contact at the lower back, and without thinking about it, do some external   squats. You will find that your movements are not particularly in synch. Repeat, but this time link arms and try and get as much contact back-to-back as you can. Both inhale, then exhale together and do an internal squat. Repeat a few times. You will find your movements are now in synch, in effect you are moving as one unit.

Also feel what is happening internally. You should feel a connection to your partner. Moving in conjunction with another person is a pleasant, relaxing experience - like in

dancing or other activities. Consider, also, what is happening here. In effect, we are combining our two separate masses into one mass and moving it.

Keep that feeling in mind. Now have your partner approach with a grab. Deflect the grab on the inside of their wrist with one hand, place your other hand to the opposite shoulder. Without breaking the flow of movement, now squat, combining your mass with your partner's as in the drill above. You should find your partner is taken down very easily, with no effort on your part. Be sure not to push down on their shoulder, don't *try* to take them down, simply let your mass connect to theirs via your hands. You can think of it like bouncing or ball, or pressing something down into water. It is a feeling of buoyancy and sinking rather than force.

Once you have this feeling, revise all the earlier takedown work putting this principle in. Of course, you can still use leverage, rotation, etc but power your movement from this internal relaxation perspective rather than just muscle. Naturally, you can add other concepts such as wave movement and spirals into this work, but the concept of internal relaxation is the most important. With a little practice you will find your work becomes more effective, more efficient and much cleaner.

Don't just work from the squat, either! Work the same procedure with push ups and sit ups too. While the squat powers takedowns, push-ups power strikes and sit-ups power ground work.

MOVEMENT
Let's also look at refining our movement. We tend to start with large, open movements in order to make everything

helps get our hands up and active, which obviously feeds in to later work.

How we initiate our movement is the subject of the next drill. We work this solo at first. Stand normally and turn your head as far as you can. At some point, this will create tension in the neck. Release the tension with movement - in other words, turn the body in the direction the heading is now facing and take a few stops. Don't stop walking until all the tension is gone and the body is re-aligned.

clear. This is also good for our health as we are stretching and opening out the body and working full range of motion in our joints. We'll begin with a footwork drill.

Three people stand in a line, about six feet apart, then begin walking. The aim is for one person to always walk through the gap between the other two. In other words, one person is always walking through the middle. In effect, everyone is walking a figure eight pattern. So you walk through the middle, turn round and walk back through the middle again. This keeps up a continuous loop of movement.

As you progress, the walkers should get closer and closer together. This forces you to refine your movement and be very precise in your steeping. In fact, see if you can move around your partners with as few steps as possible. One other thing to add in, from our previous stick drill, is to use your hand to lead you into space. This

Repeat this with all the major areas of the body. Lift and twist a shoulder, release the tension by turning and movement. Stick your chest out as far as you can, release by allowing the tension to pull your forward until re-aligned. Work from the hips, elbows, hands, knees, feet, etc. See how the tension caused by misalignment can be a prompt for the body to move.

Next, we work with a partner. Their aim is to create tension in one part of the body. This can easily be achieved by moving to punch you in the face! This should cause you to flinch. Of course, the flinch misaligns the body and creates tension. To release the tension, move as in the solo drill. In effect we are learning to recognise where tension manifests, usually due to fear or anticipation, and move to release it. Repeat will all parts of the body. Your partner might use a knife of similar to elicit a good flinch response.

Once you have that feeling, you can make your movement more tactical - move into a good space to counter or to escape. You also begin to work a little earlier, don't wait for the tension to fully develop before moving. This is a very good drill to learn how to properly use the flinch response and overcome the freeze that it normally brings.

Finally, we combine both of these drills, integrating footwork, hand position and movement. For this, our partner starts by stabbing towards us with a knife (metal training knives are best). At first, feel where the fear / tension develops in your body. It will usually be from the spot that the knife is aimed at, but not always. There then, is our prompt to move.

As that part moves, the hands should come up and one will lead into the space at the side of the knife. This, in turn, activates the feet to move. Your body adjusts it shape to fit into that safe space.

Work on the spot for a while, then add the footwork in. Take a step towards your partner, see if you can get to the side or rear of them in one or two steps. Your movement should be smooth, minimal, precise and unhurried (though it can be fast!). Once you have the idea, you can then add in your response, be it takedown, strike, etc. You can have your partner ramp up the attacks to whatever level you wish.

At the end of this process you will have developed the ability to move quickly, quietly and smoothly into the safe space from an attack, with the option to counter or escape.

FLOW
As our movements become more refined, we will also naturally begin to flow more. The notion of *flow state* or *being in the zone* is a common one in sports. It has its roots in the work of Mihaly Csikszentmihalyi, a Hungarian psychologist. Experiences in World War Two prompted him to research human happiness - *what is it that makes us happy?* One major conclusion is that we are

happiest when in flow, defined as *a state of concentration or complete absorption with the activity at hand and the situation. It is a state in which people are so involved in an activity that nothing else seems to matter.*

I'm sure that you have experienced this. You may be immersed in a book, a piece of music, in painting, in playing tennis.

Csikszentmihalyi delineated nine conditions of the flow state, as shown below. This is, of course, reducing his work to a nutshell, I would highly recommend you research further into his work as there is a wealth of interesting information there. For now, these nine conditions are a good enough starting point for our training.

If you are doing Systema reasonably well,

THE NINE CONDITIONS OF FLOW

1. Challenge-skills balance
An equal balance between skill level and challenge. If the challenge is too demanding, we get frustrated. If it is too easy, we get bored. In flow state, we feel engaged by the challenge, but not overwhelmed.

2. Action-awareness merging
We are often thinking about something that has happened, or might happen. We live in the past or the future. In flow state, we are completely absorbed in the task at hand.

3. Clear Goals
In many everyday situations, there are contradictory demands and it is sometimes unclear what should occupy our attention. However, in flow state, we have a clear purpose and good grasp of what to do next.

4. Unambiguous feedback
Direct and immediate feedback is continuously present so that we are able to constantly adjust our reactions to meet the current demands. In flow state, we know how well we are doing, all the time.

5. Concentration on the task at hand
High levels of concentration narrows our attention and excludes all unnecessary distractions. Because we are absorbed in the activity, we are only aware of what is relevant to the task at hand, and we do not think about unrelated things.

6. Sense of control
An absolute sense of personal control exists, as if we are able to do anything we want to do.

7. Loss of self-consciousness
Self-consciousness disappears. We often spend a lot of mental energy monitoring how we appear to others. In a flow state, we are too involved in the activity to care about protecting our ego.

8. Transformation of time
A distorted sense of time occurs. Time either slows down or flies by when we are completely engaged in the moment.

9. Autotelic experience
Flow is an intrinsically rewarding activity; the activity becomes autotelic, an end in itself, done for its own sake.

you should already be experiencing aspects of the flow state, especially in the more free play and sparring drills. And I use the word *free* deliberately. Flow implies movement without restriction, or impediment. We go with the flow, we don't struggle against the current.

Consider, then, what restrictions we might generally work under. Most often we impose our own on ourselves in terms of fear, tension and over-thinking. Instead, learn to let go and let your body do what it needs to do. Systema prizes instinctual reactions and natural movement above all else. This freedom to act and move is what allows us to be so fluid and adaptable in our response.

Let's start with some solo work. Take few simple movements, say, a squat, push up and a sit up. Perform one of each. No doubt you will have stopped between each exercise, changed position, then started the next movement. This is not flow.

Repeat, but this time with no pause. Transition from a low squat into your push up. From the low push up, roll over onto your back into the sit up. Repeat back through into the squat and so on. In other words, we create a chain of movements. There are individual links, or set movements, within the chain, but they are all fixed together.

From there, set yourself a time, say three minutes. Do the above movements, or any of your choice, continually for that amount of time. You can repeat each movement a few times, but you cannot pause when shifting to the next exercise. You might try going from standing to the floor, going into a side, forward and backward roll and standing up again. Or you might prefer to work with stick. Make some individual movements - a forward strike, a spin, a swing to the side. Then link them all together, let each movement feed of the previous one.

Naturally, our breathing plays a major part in this process. We should keep it in tune with the movement at first. Later, work to tune the movement to the breathing - a subtle distinction but one that improves co-ordination and flow.

There are numerous flow drills we can work with a partner. Think back to our stick disarming drill from an earlier chapter. You

panic. Post event, we carry less trauma, again we are cleaner than if still mired in fear and aggression.

It also means that we rely less on tension and local strength to win through. This is important in a self defence contact as we are likely fighting someone bigger and stronger than us. Or we may be tired, ill or injured. Any work that overly relies on a certain stance or stylise way of moving can break down if one element of the movement chain is compromised. With Systema we should be adaptable to all conditions, including our own.

Try and practice flow as often as you can. It is easily worked into everyday activities, going up the stairs, cooking, dancing, moving around. Move without pause or stutter, breathe smoothly, relax and smile!

OODA LOOP

There is one other topic I would like to cover here, as it relates to the subject of flow. I have spoken about this in other books, but will repeat the basic principles here as it is an important aspect of self defence.

The OODA Loop concept was developed by John Boyd, based on his experiences as a fighter pilot during the Korean War. In short, it breaks the decision making process down into a cycle of four stages - Observe, Orient, Decide and Act.

can work the same with a knife or similar. Your partner feeds in an attack, you neutralise, disarm and immediately return the attack. With a good partner you will quickly get into flow state, moving without thought, changing level, working smoothly. Work without resistance but don't let your partner get the upper hand. Focus on movement to achieve your goals rather than tension.

Why is this important in our work? Check through those nine conditions again. In flow state we are in the moment. This means far less, or even a total lack of, psychological stress. This means we are able to rationalise as we work and make better decisions, we are not in a blind

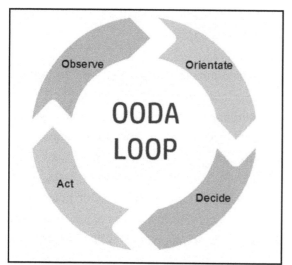

OODA LOOP

Observe

Orientate

Act

Decide

Decide - we make a decision based on the above.

Act - once the decision is made, it is acted upon.

This series of steps may take place very quickly and, it is important to note, is a loop. By that we mean that it plays continuously, each step always feeding into the next. As a simple example, you need to write something and see there is a pen on your desk. You decide to pick it up and move and act accordingly. If at some point in that process the phone rings, your loop now switches to that activity. In other words, it can be interrupted.

It came about through Boyd's experiences and observations in aerial combat, where split-second decisions are crucial. When implemented during that conflict and beyond, it led to an increase in success for pilots. Since then it has been used in military settings as well as beyond.

Let's first look at those four stages.

Observe - being aware of what is going on around you. Observe implies visual but of course our other senses are also fully involved in that process.

Orient - assessing the incoming information from the first stage. This assessment may be influenced by a number of factors, including cultural traditions, previous experience, physical make up, world-view and so on.

OODA relates to flow in two ways, In a co-operative setting, our Loops become synchronised and we flow. This might be in team work for restraint, or in playing sports or music. In an "offensive" setting we use it to break the attacker's flow of thought and movement, giving us a gap in which to work

This is where it becomes important for self defence. A simple example, again. An attacker observes you and you annoy them, for some reason. They process information such as distance, chance of success, etc and make a decision to punch you. They then begin to act on that decision, and move in to punch. If, as they do so, you change position, or throw out a kick to their knee, they have to pause, re-observe, orient, etc. In other words, you can knock them back to the beginning of the loop.

Now, we have to be aware that we are talking fractions of a second here, but nonetheless even that small amount of time can be vital. You can think of it as keeping a person physically off-balance. If someone comes in to grab your arm, offer it then, just as they touch, move it away along the direction of their movement. Chances are they will either follow, as they expected support, so losing balance, or they will have to re-adjust, giving you time to respond.

Training in this begins with our earlier pre-emptive drills, where we learn to recognise an attack at its earliest stage. If we can cut into the person's movement at the point, they will have to reset their loop.

Don't think this is just physical, either.

There is usually a verbal component to any physical confrontation. It might be insults it might be what is called "interviewing." A person is sounding you out as a potential victim, perhaps. Also, it is surprising how many people work to a script. This is where certain actions or words always get certain results. If that result is not forthcoming, there is a break in the loop, the person has to reset. A bit like walking down the stairs and there is one more than you expected!

We can also use the OODA Loop in these situations. The most recognised way is by asking a question, as this engages the brain for a second. It is good to ask a "visual" question as this tends to occupy the eyes for an instant- eye access cues are another interesting areas of study.

Try it with a partner. Get them to act confrontational, then ask "what colour are your socks?" Watch the eyes. Chances are, if you haven't told them what the drill is, that they will be absent for a second, giving you a space in which to work.

Imagine firing questions at someone. You never quite give them the chance to answer before you bark the next question. How many people would pass exams under those conditions? This may work in a situation by shouting out orders at someone, particularly if you are in an authoritative position.

We can combine the two, of course. One way to test this out, is to ask your partner a question and, as they go to answer, slap them in the face. It's a good example of how to break the OODA Loop but I'm not responsible for any fallout!

To return to our physical work, experiment with different ways of interrupting the loop during drills. It doesn't even have to involve contact, just the threat of contact. As the person approaches, a sudden movement to the knees or groin may cause a flinch. Slightly repositioning yourself also gives out subtle signals that can interrupt the loop.

So a working knowledge of the OODA Loop can help us keep at least one step ahead. Watch for it in everyday life. You might see how a person at work maintains control of a meeting by interrupting other people's loops , for example. In fact, Boyd later applied his work to the corporate world, expanding it way beyond its original application. After all, human nature is human nature whatever the situation.

INSTINCT

We spoke in an earlier chapter about instinct and described some drills. The first step to tapping into our innate instinct is to be attentive. Even just practicing our solo

exercises with a focus on breathing will bring significant results. Through this, we begin to establish a "base-line" feeling for our internal state. We should then instantly notice when we start to become stressed, anxious, tense and so on. You would be surprised how many people are unaware of their tension. This is largely because the stressful condition has become normalised in industrialised society - we are supposed to be worried, about money, about or status, about our job. This has led to an astronomic rise in stress-related conditions, on top of which we now have the pandemic to deal with. Just look at newspaper headlines, they are all designed to push your stress buttons.

Recognising this and monitoring your personal stress levels already goes a long way to putting you back in touch with your primal self. These are not skills we are developing - as we often say, Systema reminds us what it is to be a fully functional human being.

From there, how can we work to refine our intuitive state? We mentioned blindfold drills before, these are one of the best methods, as they rely largely on feel. I say feel, because that is the sensation we get. Some experience a tingling in the skin, particularly between the shoulder blades if approached from behind.

As mentioned before, scientists place the figure of our senses as high as twelve, or even more. Many of these relate to our internal state, hunger, temperature, proprioception, balance and so on. Also, some of our receptors are used for more than one sense. Retinas, for example, are portals for the light waves we need for vision, but some retinal cells also inform the brain if it's daytime or night time. This unnamed day/night sense is the basis for circadian rhythms that affect our metabolism and sleep/wake cycle.

In fact, when we look into it deeper, we find that our brain constructs everything we see, hear, smell, taste and feel using more than just the sense data from the body's receptors. Light waves, for example, don't simply enter your eyes, travel to your brain as electrical signals, and then you see. Your brain actually predicts what you might see before you see it, based on past experience, the state of your body and your current situation. It combines its predictions with the incoming sense data from your retinas to construct your visual experience of the world around you.

Similarly, when you place your fingers on your wrist to feel your pulse, you're actually feeling a construction based on your brain's predictions and the actual sense data. We don't experience sensations with our sense organs, we experience them with brain. How important, then, that we are able to process information provided by the brain in an efficient and calm way. Tension, fear, anger, all add static or noise to our internal signals, a bit like trying to hear a whispered conversation at a rock concert. Control of our emotional state improves internal communication of all kinds.

There are many variations on the blindfold

drill - you can add in a knife for extra intent, you can turn all the lights off and play hide and seek! I always find that these "childish" games, particularly when done outdoors at night, touch people very deeply. I mentioned the word primal before, I think this type of activity connects us directly to our hunter/gatherer ancestors, whose daily survival relied on their instinct and abilities.

Another practice to consider, then, is spending time outdoors in nature. Today, even when people go for a walk or a jog, they are plugged in, to an MP3 player or phone. Leave them at home! As we said before, walk or jog with a full awareness of what is around you. Be observant across all your senses, take the time to pause and examine now and then. You might be surprised at what you haven't noticed before, even on a familiar route.

In terms of self defence, we can apply our base-line principle to human behaviour. It should be easy to distinguish between a group of people having a good time and a group involved in an argument - we know the indicators. But take it deeper than that. See if you can pick this information up before the more overt indicators begin. Can you feel a change in atmosphere? Can you feel if someone is staring at you with bad intent?

Gavin Becker wrote about this in his excellent book *The Gift of Fear*. In brief, he researched people who had been subject to sexual assault. He found that in the vast majority of cases, the person felt that something was wrong, prior to the assault. Sad to say, also in many cases, they failed to act on this information - perhaps largely due to social pressures around "not making a fuss." It may be a generalisation, but I've found that women are often more attuned to this inner voice than men - maybe because of the type of situation they have to deal with on a more regular basis.

Another way to enhance this ability is to work drills that give little or no time for thought. Simply throwing and catching a stick is a good example. Start in pairs, throwing the stick back and forth (*to* each other, not *at* each other!). Gradually increase the group size until you have six or so people throwing a catching one stick.

Next, gradually add in three more sticks, one at a time. So eventually you have a group of six or so people moving around the space catching and throwing four sticks. The general awareness benefits, in terms of peripheral vision and placement should be obvious. But go deeper. When engaged in the drill, learn to let go with he brain and let the body move of its own accord - you will be surprised how often the body predicts where the next stick is coming from without much apparent external information.

WIDER SELF DEFENCE

We should also broaden out or idea of self defence beyond our immediate physical situation. We can think if home security, on-line security, and so on. As the hold of technology increases, so do the opportunities for those savvy enough to hack into it. Take time to review your home. Do you have decent locks on the doors and windows? What are the obvious entry / exit points? Are they secure?

Security cameras are readily available these days, that transmit direct to your phone. It is also worth contacting your local police station. Most forces in the UK have a dedicated Crime Reduction team that will give you free advice on home and personal security.

Make sure you have all the latest and relevant protections in place on your computers / phone. Be aware of using wi-fi in public places, look into using VPNs to cover yourself in such situations. Again, it is best to consult a professional in the field to get the best current advice.

Another wider issue to consider is lifestyle. Do you keep getting into lots of fights and arguments? Perhaps you hang out in seedy bars frequented by drunks and drug dealers (in other words you are a musician lol). Perhaps you have toxic people in your life who bring nothing but negativity? Is your

someone has invented an app for this! Build a format for your reports. You might want to include:
Time and place
Particular conditions
Actions of others
How did that make me feel?
Stress scale of 1-5, where 1 is "peeved" and 5 is "bloody furious!"
Was the situation resolved?

job, or lack of a job, causing undue amounts of stress?

A good first step to defending against stress and aggravation is to review your lifestyle. This widens our work out a little into the area of stress management, another deep subject, but here's a very simple exercise that will get you started.

A journal can be a great tool for helping pinpoint stress triggers. It doesn't have to be particularly complex or detailed, just keep a note of how you have felt on a particular day. For example: *Monday - 8.15am drove into work. Roadworks, heavy rain. Got agitated waiting in traffic queue.* It can be as simple as that.

Where possible, try to add to your journal as soon as possible after the event. You don't even have to write it, you could record on your phone or similar. Perhaps

Over even a short period of time, you will quickly build up a "stress picture." Looking back over it, you can hopefully begin to pick out patterns, those particular situations and issues that are most likely to act as triggers. Next, make a list of these issues, again, keep it simple, it might be just one word - *boss!*

Go through the list and put each item into one of two categories - CAN and CAN'T.

Can are things we can change or do something about. Can't are things we have little or no control over. Ignore those for the moment. Return to your Can list. What can you change for the better in each of these cases? You could stop going to that bar. You could work to distances yourself from those negative people. You could speak to your HR department about that difficult person, or perhaps look to transfer or change jobs.

The next stage is to act on those changes. You don't have to do all of them at once! In some cases, breaking habits is difficult, so don't pressure yourself too much. But do make progress, however slow. You will hopefully reap the rewards in terms of less stress and aggravation in your life.

Also, don't forget to make time for yourself, even if it's only five minutes a day sitting somewhere quiet. Reducing stress will have a dramatic positive effect on all aspects of your health, a prime consideration in self defence.

TESTING & SCENARIOS

We return to the physical for our final topic. Throughout, we have mentioned the idea of testing our work. After all, how can we be sure that those skills we demonstrate so well with a friendly partner will hold up under real world pressure?

Everything needs to be tested. In some ways we can do this through our regular drills, applying the Ten Points principle described earlier. Simply start turning up the volume on each of the points - go faster, add restrictions, and so on. But these are still training drills, usually to develop attributes. We need also to apply these attributes into situations in order to test them.

The first thing to determine is what exactly do we want to test? We can then set up our exercise from there. It may be that we want to test an attribute, a technical skill, mindset and emotional control, or the general ability to apply work according to the demands of the situation. We also need a way of judging the test, of assessing success or failure, or anywhere between the two. Setting clear goals will help with this - if the aim is to hit a target five times in 30 seconds, success or failure is quite clear. In other cases, it might be more a case of assessing a person's reaction to events.

It is also a good idea to give a safe word on any drill. If a person says this, the drill ends immediately. This is very important for some of the more intense and demanding testing work we carry out.

Let's start with testing an attribute, say movement. The set up is that A has to avoid contact with B. One clear way of assessing results would be to give B a marker pen and have A wear a white T-shirt. We next set up the test parameters and assign tasks to the people involved. So in this case, it is B's job to try and "slash or stab" with the pen as though it were a knife. The test for A is to evade only (they are not allowed to block or fight back). We then set a time limit - say one minute - and establish any other variables such as speed, start distance, training area (confined or open).

In terms of equipment we of course need a marker pen, a white T-shirt and would also advise eye protection. Place A and B in start positions and go. After the time is up it is easy to count the amount of slashes / stabs that got through. We can re-run the same drill with different variables. Use a different coloured marker so we can still count the hits. Start from a different distance, or allow A to try and block / deflect the attacks for example. Once again, we can clearly see the results.

We may wish to test a skill such as escaping from a lock or hold. In this case A's job is to apply the lock as best they can. We can then give B a set time to try and escape. Again, failure or success can easily be seen, B escapes or they do not. Variables can include the use, or not, of striking and levels of resistance.

This type of testing doesn't have to be overly physical. We can put someone under intense psychological pressure using shouting, slaps, forced breath holds and similar. Again, put a time limit on the drill and make it clear that the aim for the person is to endure the experience while maintaining calm, not to fight their way out.

Our next method of testing is goal-oriented sparring. As mentioned before, the word sparring usually conjures up a sports-based setting. Instead, each person in these drills has a specific goal to achieve particular to the setting. Here is an example.

A is in the centre of the room. B (plus optional C and/or D) has to get A out

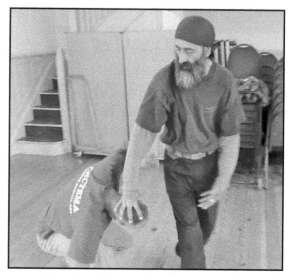

208

attacks someone. The two security partners must as quickly possible protect the target and disarm and restrain the attacker. This calls not only for restraint skills, but also observation and awareness and communication. The smart security people will have some ideas prepared on how to work best as a team. As before, we impose a time limit and, of course, swap around roles regularly. Also consider that it isn't just the two security people that should be exercising awareness, everyone without a knife should be, too!

through the door at the end of the room. They have a set time to do this, say 90 seconds. The parameters of the drill are set - B is not allowed to punch or kick unless A does, and then it must be a proportionate response, etc.

Protective gear is optional, though its protective effects must be taken into considerations. By that, I mean a full power hit to the head must be treated as such, even if it bounces off a padded helmet. So, set the drill, put the people in position, makes sure they understand the rules, and off we go.

From here, we can start to work into full situational testing. This widens our sparring out into more of a real-life situation. For example - set up a group so that we have six or so people as "the crowd" and two people as "the security." Everyone moves around, then at some point one of the crowd pulls a knife and

This brings us into the area of scenarios. These, when set up well, are an excellent way to test skills and also give people the chance to integrate and apply all the things they have been learning. They can be as simple as the previous knife attack scenario or they can be extremely involved and extend across quite a time. In the past, we have run a scenario drill over a weekend, involving escape, evasion and many other things. This will often depend on time, resources and logistics, but it is possible to run quite extensive scenarios with good preparation and a team of people assisting.

All of the previous training variations come into play with scenarios, though normally we are working to keep things at real life speed

settings you have access to for training. If we are running a road rage scenario, for example, it makes sense to work in and around cars. As much as possible we try to fit the setting to the situation. I mentioned before a workshop we held in a local social club - we had a dance floor, lounge area and bar to work in. Other venues have included car parks, an industrial unit and a swimming pool!

EQUIPMENT

This includes weapons, improvised or other, or any items relevant to the situation. It also includes clothing. So if you are simulating a situation in a park in January it makes sense for people to be wearing overcoats (at least in the UK!)

SCRIPT

In most scenarios, one or more people will have a specific task and so will be running to a script. In the case of our road rage example, we may prime Mr Angry to be annoyed that you have just nudged his rear bumper at the traffic lights. His script is to jump out of his car and angrily approach you with lots of swearing and aggression. How you react is up to you.

PARAMETERS

It is a good idea to set some parameters to a script. Continuing the road rage example, it may be that we set Mr Angry to back down if you confront him. It may be that he is set

and levels of resistance. Contact levels can be adjusted to suit, with the caveat that strikes or similar must be acknowledged. We need to avoid things like people ignoring knife strikes, or, as I remember seeing once in paintball, someone wiping off the paint when they had been shot! For a general scenario framework, think of these factors:

SITUATION

What kind of situation are you trying to recreate? As a starting point we usually use the experiences of people in the class, or you can try some of the earlier incidents in this book. The most common of these are road rage, a fight in or outside a pub, attempted robbery, a domestic dispute, helping someone in trouble.

SETTING

The next thing to consider is what kind of

up to physically attack you whatever your response. We also need to set some time limit or conditions for success to a drill as well. Most fights or arguments are over in a few minutes and we need to reflect this in the drill. It may also be that the "defender" in the scenario has a particular function to fulfil too - it may be the defence of another, or working within a set of legal or professional restrictions.

ROLE PLAY

Scenario work calls for an element of role play. This can be an issue when everyone knows each other and even the heaviest verbal aggression can be taken lightly. There is very little you can do about this, except make the situation as real as possible. Try to pair people who don't know each other so well, or use outside people.

In the past, for our longer scenarios, we have been able to bring in outsiders, such as a couple of friends of who kindly stepped in as "angry farmers" for one particular exercise. Even though everyone knew we were training, we were able to add a huge amount of uncertainty into the proceedings which certainly added to the experience!

In the usual scenarios we are often calling for a person to be aggressive and intimidating, though this is not always the case. Sometimes we may ask a person to

be "procedural" or to act scared or frightened depending on the aims of the drill. Not everyone in the drill has to be an attacker. It may be we have to protect or help someone in difficulty, for example, which then gives us something else to deal with as they hang on to our arm as we work against the attacker!

WHAT IF?

A common question in martial arts... *what if?* Well with a good framework for developing scenarios you can answer almost anything. Though I draw the line at one (serious!) question I got when showing knife disarms, "what if he has a light sabre." I suppose I should have answered "shoot him with my phaser."

That aside, it's good to explore all these different possibilities through scenario work, so don't be afraid to re-run scenarios with slightly tweaked parameters. While we generally keep to basic situations it is also fun to occasionally break into more "interesting" realms, though you have to be careful you don't get too carried away, unless you particularly enjoy Live Action Role Playing, I guess!

OUTCOMES AND ANALYSIS

Any scenario work should be followed by a de-brief or circle up once finished. It is important to point out that there is not necessarily one right way to deal with a particular situation. Running the scenario a few times allows you to explore different approaches and outcomes. It may be best to escape the situation and area, it may be best to ignore the other person, or to calm them down, or to take some direct physical action.

Some scenarios are more about surviving the situation and or controlling our fear response than any particular physical action. It is important that the people taking part understand this. No-one should be under the illusion they are required to be a "tough guy" in every situation. Being low key may be the most important thing, or if you are with family member for example, getting them clear of the trouble zone.

We should always have an eye on realism too, both in terms of physical capabilities and in terms of consequences, legal and otherwise. Alongside this, there should be a thorough safety assessment prior to running any drill, particularly when working outside of the regular class environment. Ensure everyone is briefed exactly on what the scenario involves and that there is a very clear signal to start and end (I usually use a whistle). On hearing the whistle everyone should stop immediately. Likewise, remember to give people a method of indicating if they wish to leave a drill. They should be free to do so at any point, without judgement.

Having set all those factors in place, let's run through a few ideas. These are extremely typical scenarios, perhaps even a

212

bit clichéd, but they do reflect real life experiences and serve as a good starting point for developing your own ideas.

ROBBERY

Situation: A is standing at a cash point withdrawing money. B approaches and asks for money.

Setting: can be run in regular class, the "cash point" is a radiator or something similar

Equipment: knives for the attacker/s

Script: B can be a homeless guy after money for a cup of tea, a drug addict, a nervous robber, an aggressive robber prepared to use violence.

What if: there is more than one attacker - attacker/s have knives - A has a friend passing by - A has a child with them

ROAD RAGE

Situation: A has just parked in a car park. It seems they have stolen B's parking space

Setting: A is sitting in their car, B approaches on foot

Equipment: B may have an improvised weapon, perhaps something normally carried in a car.

Script: B is angry!

What if: attacker has a friend who joins in - A has family in the car - A has access to improvised weapons - B is armed - the car door is un/locked, windows closed / open

- there is CCTV covering the area

RESCUE

Situation: A is walking through the park. They see B holding a knife to C's throat

Setting: outdoors, or may be run in regular class

Equipment: a knife

Script: - B is trying to rob C - B is trying to move C to another location - B is known to C and is righting some perceived wrong - B has psychological issues

What if: A has a dog - C is active or passive - the police arrive as A is punching B - B has an accomplice

DID YOU SPILL MY PINT?

Situation: A is in or outside a pub and accidentally bumps into B

Setting: a pub setting, or a room with furniture / confined spaces

Equipment: plastic glasses

Script: B pushes back and becomes immediately aggressive - B is annoyed but may be calmed down

the course of one of our camps. We won't go into full details here, but give you an outline of one part, which hopefully will give you some ideas on how to create a more involved scenario

What if: B has three friends who immediately gather round - A has three friends who immediately gather round! - there are several people who will watch but not get involved.

DRUNKEN UNCLE
Situation: At a family wedding Uncle Bill has had too much to drink and is arguing with Uncle Frank. A has to intervene and manage the situation.
Setting: a bar setting, or a room with furniture / confined spaces
Equipment: plastic glasses
Script: the uncles shout but don't come to blows - they push and shove or go into a full fight - A has to work without hurting anyone!
What if: other family members join in - one uncle has a medical episode, eg heart attack (once again not all scenarios need be about fighting.)

EVASION
This was an extensive drill carried out over

Situation: the entire group has been captured, restrained, blindfolded and confined, placed in stress positions. After a while they are placed into a vehicle and driven to an unknown location (a field a couple of miles away). They are led into the field then "something happens" and their captor is no longer there. They have a map and now have an opportunity to get back to a safe location (marked on the map).

In the meantime, captors are patrolling the area in vehicles trying to spot the escapees.
Setting: countryside, or could be run in an urban setting. Be sure to have landowner's permission where appropriate. We also advised locals that an exercise was taking place (using public footpaths for the most part).

It may also help if you have good contacts or connections in the local police in order to avoid any problems (unless you want to make those part of the scenario!)
Equipment: vehicles, blindfolds, map.
Script: some captors patrol in vehicles and can relay sighting to captors on foot -

escapees are captured by any simple physical contact from captors (eg a hand on the shoulder) - no resistance is allowed once captured, you are to get into the vehicle

What if: there are people around who will assist the escapees - there are people around who will hinder the escapees - you encounter an angry farmer!

These are just a few scenario ideas to get you started. The best scenarios are based on real life experiences, so ask your group for ideas. Don't get caught up in the "attacker defender" mode all the time - some situations are not so cut and dry. Imagine a police scenario where the officer arrives during an altercation and has no idea what is going on. Similarly not every scenario needs to be a fight - you can incorporate medical / first aid situations, awareness and escape, emergencies, close protection, basically anything that will put people under pressure.

A scenario, or any testing drill, should always be closely monitored in order to ensure everything is running as it should, things are safe and people are coping well enough with the pressure. At any point if you have any doubt, stop the drill immediately. For larger scenarios, or even normal size ones, it is good to have one or more people other than the instructor monitoring, too. This in itself

can be a good test of observation skills.

How often you run scenarios is up to you. We don't do them that often and when we do they are usually part of a workshop on a specific topic, such as in-car defence. After a day's training it gives people a nice opportunity to try out some of the things they have learnt. I think if you run scenarios too often they tend to lose impact and also the class risks coming more of an Am Dram session!

By the same token, taking the class out of the training hall and into some woods, a car park or any other "unusual" area can often provide new challenges and so accelerate learning. Even if you are not running scenarios, I would always recommend taking the class out of the usual training environment whenever you can. It opens up many more possibilities, not just for

ground, for example. Some areas require a full book in themselves and, over time, we plan to release titles on as many of these topics as we can.

However, if you take the base Systema principles, with a little work you can fit them into any situation. And, of course, there are numerous other book and film resources available should you need further guidance.

application work, but for general exercise, getting used to working in the cold or wet, developing specific skills such as woodcraft, orientation, etc, We generally get a better feeling of working in the real word as opposed to a sterile training area. So keep it real, keep it safe and, above all have fun while learning!

CONCLUSIONS

There ends our look at Systema self defence. I hope you find some things in this book that are useful not only in your training but in your daily life and activities.

As I mentioned at the start, self defence can cover so many situations, physical and non-physical, that no single book could do justice to the topic. I apologise if I have repeated any drills or info during the book and also for any omissions - we have not particularly covered fighting on the

I have quite few families come to me for self defence training, particularly with issues such as bullying, knife crime and county lines drug gangs so prominent in the news. It's aways a fine balance between making people, particularly young people, aware of the dangers, and scaring them into deep paranoia. I feel that the Systema approach achieves this balance particularly well, given its emphasis on both the psychological and physical aspects of confrontation.

If you are teaching your own children, or other young people, please bear this balance in mind. Self defence training seems to vary between taking no physical action at all (from a belief that you can always talk your way out, which is somewhat naive at best) to all-out feral, ultra-combatives blasting away (which, aside from other questions, often appears to do more damage to the participants than anyone else.) Train with realism but also train with humour, humility and with an open mind. Be creative and adaptive and always work to benefit your own well-being and that of the people closest to you.

Whether you train in Systema or just wish to apply some of its principles to your own art or style, always consider the professional mindset. How do top tier people operate, in any activity? With calm, cold efficiency. They work *clean.*

The world is a dangerous place, for some of us it is also safer than it ever has been. That is not the case globally, unfortunately, and we now appear to be facing wider threats, in terms of resources, pollution and climate. As humans we are able to think ahead, construct possible scenarios and plan accordingly. That goes for the micro and macro level.

On the micro, you might be a tourist in a strange area. As we said before, keep your valuables hidden away, try and blend in. On the macro - there may be the prospect of power cuts over the coming months. Buy a torch and some candles (don't forget the matches!). That is not being a "conspiracy nut", that is basic preparation.

As I hope you have seen, Systema principles can be scaled up or down according to the situation. Sometimes it is just a case of "preparing to be prepared." Other times, we plan ahead for something specific. Then, unfortunately, there are always those situations where we get caught on the hop and have to improvise. In each case, if you have put in the training and have gained the understanding, you will be as best equipped as you can be to deal with anything.

Thank you, again, to my teachers Mikhail and Vladimir, all those others I've had the opportunity to train under and to my own students, particularly the regulars who have supported the club during a difficult time. If you have any questions, or suggestions for future books or films, please do drop me a line via the contract details overleaf.

Stay safe.

NOTES

NOTES

NOTES

RESOURCES

Systema HQ Moscow   www.systemaryabko.com

Systema HQ Toronto   www.russianmartialart.com

Cutting Edge Systema   www.systemauk.com

                                             E-mail systemauk@outlook.com

Systema books & Instructional films www.systemafilms.com

General health books and films   www.simplyflow.myshopify.com

Health training   www.simplyflow.co.uk

RECOMMENDED READING

Strikes - Vladimir Vasiliev & Scott Meredith

Let Every Breath - Vladimir Vasiliev

Secrets of the Russian Blade Masters - Vladimir Vasiliev

The Systema Manual - Major Konstantin Komarov

The Gift of Fear - Gavin Becker

Other books by Robert Poyton:

Systema Solo Training

Systema Partner Training

Systema Awareness Training

Systema Voices

Systema Locks, Holds and Throws

Systema for Seniors

Fitness Over 40

Don't Worry - A Guide to Stress Management

The Eight Brocades Qigong Exercise

Lightning Source UK Ltd.
Milton Keynes UK
UKHW050211260122
397668UK00013B/287